sexual
intimacy
for women

A Guide for Same-Sex Couples

sexual intimacy for women

A Guide for Same-Sex Couples

DR. GLENDA CORWIN

SEAL PRESS

Sexual Intimacy for Women
A Guide for Same-Sex Couples

Published by Seal Press
A Member of the Perseus Books Group
1700 Fourth Street
Berkeley, CA 94710

Library of Congress Cataloging-in-Publication Data:

Corwin, Glenda.
  Sexual intimacy for women : a guide for same-sex couples / by Glenda Corwin.
    p. cm.
  ISBN 978-1-58005-303-7
  1. Sex instruction for lesbians. 2. Lesbians--Sexual behavior. 3. Lesbian couples. I. Title.
  HQ75.51.C67 2010
  613.9'6086643--dc22
                                        2009025402

9 8 7 6 5 4 3

Cover Design: Domini Dragoone
Interior Design: Megan Jones Design
Printed in the United States of America
Distributed by Publishers Group West

The information in this book is intended to help readers make informed decisions about their health and well-being, and the health and well-being of loved ones. It is not intended to be a substitute for treatment by or the advice and care of a licensed health care provider or mental health professional. While the authors and publisher have endeavored to ensure that the information presented is accurate and up-to-date, they shall not be held responsible for loss or damage of any nature suffered as a result of reliance on any of this book's contents or any errors or omissions herein.

To all the women who talked with me about sex and intimacy, and their hopes for more.

contents

Introduction

As WOMEN WHO love women, we remember how we started this journey. Each of us can recall the first time we knew, accepted, and, perhaps, revealed sexual attraction to another woman. Most of us can vividly remember the overwhelming erotic excitement of our first lesbian sexual encounter: the *Aha!* moment of it, the anticipation of getting to have sex with women for the rest of our lives if we so choose, or the special feelings of pride and kinship that often come with coming out.

The entire experience leaves us with our hearts full and our heads spinning—which makes it all the more sad and ironic when we eventually catch wind of what feels like the dirty little secret of the lesbian world.

Some of us first hear about it through the grapevine; some of us first discover it, alas, through personal experience. Some of us meet lesbian couples who have been together for decades, perhaps peacefully . . . but platonically. And we find out that it's *apparently* so common that there is even a name for it: "lesbian bed death."

And we wonder, *Do I have to give up passion in exchange for stability?*

ONCE WE START asking ourselves that question, others start to pop up as well, especially if we are still emotionally attached to our partner and want to make the relationship work:

1

Does sex really matter that much anyway?

Why place such emphasis on a few minutes of sexual contact?

Why focus on the bedroom when there's so much more to intimate relationships: affection, companionship, family ties?

While it's true that sex isn't everything, it *is* something—something important, even vital, to who we are. It improves the quality of our lives, and when it comes to long-term partnerships, sexual intimacy helps maintain a special bond, through thick and thin.

When straight women say, "We haven't had sex in forever," they usually mean several months. Lesbians saying that often mean several years. We tend to be rather complacent about our sex lives, especially if we're otherwise satisfied with our relationship. It's unfortunate that so many of us are prone to focusing only on "affection" and "companionship," as wonderful as those things are. I understand, of course, it may feel safer and more socially acceptable to focus on those things. But by ignoring the sexual aspect of a relationship, we're missing an important point.

When you were discovering your attraction to women, it was probably something amazing. That excitement was strong enough to propel you past the fears and obstacles that so often come with this discovery. You could have avoided it all and lived a heterosexual life, befriending women and partnering only with men. But you didn't, for certain reasons—sexual reasons. Straight women enjoy deep and loving relationships with other women, but they're not lovers. They may hug and cuddle, but they don't feel drawn toward sexual contact with each other. It is our sexual interest in women is that makes us different. And that's why we need to make it a point of focus.

I'VE BEEN PRACTICING as an openly lesbian psychologist for more than twenty years. In that time, I've listened to hundreds of my female clients—not to mention friends and colleagues—lament the loss of sexual intimacy in their same-sex relationships. Some of them have ended relationships over this issue, and many others have settled into silent, sexless stalemates.

Some people say that most women in same-sex relationships aren't bothered by a lack of sexual intimacy; that we're fine with not being very sexual. I don't believe that. I'm not fine with being asexual, and neither are the majority of women I know. Furthermore, in 2007 I conducted an online survey of sexual patterns in female same-sex relationships.[1] In the survey, 90 percent of the 400 respondents said they believed regular sexual contact was important in a primary relationship. In follow-up interviews with thirty of those women, all of them said sex can bring a closer and deeper connection with a partner. They said that sex was very important to them, even though many hadn't had sex with their partners in months or even years. Furthermore, the women who were not sexually active with their partners said that they never attempted to plan time for sexual intimacy, thinking that would be too "contrived." I was struck by the dichotomy: Such high value is placed on sexual intimacy, but apparently, so little is done to nurture it.

Why is that? If we already know that sex is important, why don't we practice what we preach? I've heard the answer again and again, in hundreds of therapy sessions and in conversations with other women: Most of us simply don't know how to maintain sexual intimacy over the long term.

Now on the one hand, it's hard to imagine why, in this day and age, women don't do more to take matters into their own hands and find out how to solve this kind of problem in their lives. But not so fast. Choosing to sustain a sexually active relationship is not easy. It often requires that we confront fears, challenge long-held beliefs, and totally change our approach to sex. Then add the fact that we're immersed in antisexual, antifemale, and antilesbian myths and attitudes, and that many of us also have our own internalized self-limiting beliefs that leave us feeling inadequate, ashamed, or guilty about our sexual behavior. It's no wonder so many women do not actively engage in finding a solution, and that so many eventually give up entirely. This kind of work takes a lot of courage. But it's courage you have. Remember: It took tremendous courage to accept your attraction to women in the first place. You've proven your strength.

If you're having doubts about whether it is worth the effort, think about the times you've felt real *passion*—that blend of love and sexual excitement that connects you to another person, and to yourself, in the deepest way possible. Or think about a time when pure lust sent you into sexual orbit, and you felt completely absorbed and thrilled with physical pleasure.

You deserved to have those experiences, and you still deserve to have them, again and again. When reading this book, I hope you'll let those memories remind you of what you have to gain by taking some of these risks and doing some things that are very hard for most of us to do. You'll have to go deep inside yourself, and let yourself act in ways you weren't trained to act, being vulnerable, honest, selfish, and even "naughty" as you share the full range of sexual experience with another person. Not only will these new skills enhance your sexual relationships, but they'll probably enhance your relationships with many other people in your life. You can only benefit from dealing with your fears and strengthening your ability to be vulnerable, honest, and, yes, even "selfish."

I know it's possible to keep sexual passion alive. I've talked with many women who do preserve a passionate connection and who protect this precious aspect of their relationship. In my experience, about 20 percent of lesbian couples who live together meet the criteria that sex therapists use to define a "sexually active" (SA) couple: They have sexual contact at least twice a month.

What's their secret? These SA women are very *intentional* about their sexual relationships, protecting their privacy and time for intimate focus on each other. They take responsibility for their own sexuality, consciously engaging in thoughts and activities that make them feel more sexual. They also pay attention to how they can support or sabotage each other in the sexual arena, and they work as a team to create conditions that are conducive to sexual intimacy. These are practices that all women can learn and apply to their own lives, and that's where this book comes in.

Sexual Intimacy for Women is for women who love women and want to keep sexual passion alive in their intimate relationships. Chapters 1 and 2 deal with sexual desire. In that section, I dispel the myths and reveal the truths about female sexuality; I also explain the important difference between spontaneous and responsive desire.

The remaining chapters focus on common conflicts and their solutions, using both explanation and example—that is, personal stories—to illustrate my points. Every personal story in the book has been carefully edited to protect confidentiality. In fact, some stories represent composites of different women with similar concerns. You will not recognize a specific individual in these pages—but you may recognize yourself. It's highly likely you'll be able to relate to one or more personal stories that pepper this book. Through the examples in these stories, you may see ways that you are limiting your own capacity for full sexual relationships.

Chapters 3 through 8 are each focused on a different stumbling block, the most ubiquitous being a discrepancy in desire levels between partners. Of those chapters, you may want to skip to those that are pertinent for you. But make sure to read every bit of chapters 9 through 12, each of which address a vital component of maintaining and deepening sexual intimacy.

Can passion thrive after novelty fades? Can you choose to be long-term lovers instead of platonic partners? The answer is a resounding *yes*. Armed with this book and a little determination, you can challenge your own personal obstacles to sexual passion and start to change the beliefs and behaviors that deprive you of this wonderful gift.

DR. GLENDA CORWIN

just the facts:
women, sex, and desire

1

Women and Sex: Separating Fact from Fiction

WHEN IT COMES to sex, women are burdened by so many falsehoods—about how much desire we should have, how quickly we should get aroused, how much sex we should be having with our partners, how long it should take to have an orgasm . . . the list goes on.

It's tragic, because these false beliefs can be limiting, even paralyzing. Women who compare themselves to fictional standards of peak sexual performance feel inadequate, which in turn lowers their sexual self-esteem and makes them avoid intimate connections. For example, I often hear women say they have a "low sex drive"—implying "lower than normal." But do they actually know what is statistically normal? Usually not. When I tell these women what *is* statistically normal, they often realize that their sex drive is actually about average. This realization comes with a big boost to their self-esteem, as they think, *Nothing is wrong with me after all!*

Though being happy is much more important than being "statistically normal," knowing what *is* normal helps. Accurate information about sex can be liberating: Energy and attention can be shifted away from imaginary deficits and can then be directed toward positive options. Even if the truth turns out to confirm our suspicions, it's still empowering, because knowledge about an issue helps us to stop ruminating about it. From there, we can let it go or take action to remedy it. The choice is ours.

In my sexual-intimacy workshops and consultations, I've found that there are certain beliefs about women's desire that tend to come up very often. I've listed them in this chapter, and addressed each one with the facts.

Some of the beliefs have to do with female desire in general, and others have to do with women in same-sex relationships. While reading this chapter, you may start to think that the research cited for the former seems stronger than that cited for the latter. You'd be right. While there is sufficient information on female desire, there is an unfortunate deficit of contemporary hard research about women in same-sex relationships. There are multiple online surveys, but it's hard to generalize from these because the samples may be very skewed. Women who respond to online sex surveys may be different from women who don't; for instance, they may be more interested in sex than women who don't respond to the same survey. In order to draw up-to-date conclusions about the sexual behavior of women in same-sex relationships, we have to take information from old research studies and combine that data with what little current evidence we have—such as online surveys and clinical and anecdotal experiences—to make some estimations. It's not ideal, but it's satisfactory, and for now, it's all we've got.

As you'll see, a few of the common beliefs actually *do* seem to be confirmed by research evidence. But I'm betting you'll be surprised about how many are not, and that you'll be relieved and empowered by much of what you read here.

"Long-term lesbian couples are less sexual than long-term heterosexual couples."

In the '80s we had some widely accepted scientific evidence that this was true. In 1982, University of Washington sociologists Philip Blumstein and Pepper Schwartz surveyed 22,000 American couples—straight, lesbian, and gay male—and asked how frequently they "had sex relations" with each other.[1] Overall, Blumstein and Schwartz found that gay men were the most sexually active, followed by heterosexual couples, and then, lastly, lesbian couples. Among couples together for more than two years, more than 50 percent of lesbian couples had sex less than once a month, whereas only 15 percent of heterosexual couples had sex less than once a month. After living together more than ten years, 85 percent of lesbian and 33 percent of heterosexual couples reported sex less than once a month, if at all.

Interestingly, all couples reported a fairly similar frequency of "sex relations" in the first two years of their relationship. After that point, however, the lesbian couples' frequency slowed down much more dramatically than that of gay male and heterosexual couples. Sex therapist Marny Hall called this "the third-year plunge"[2] in lesbian sexual frequency—an apt phrase for a very observable phenomenon.

Some researchers have argued that the Blumstein and Schwartz study imposed a too-narrow definition of sexuality, and that this could have skewed the results for same-sex female couples, whose "sex relations" could be seen to include a wider range of activities. But that doesn't make sense to me. Do kissing and cuddling constitute "sex relations?" I don't think so, and I don't think most women do. In my experience, when women talk about sex, they usually mean something that involves genital stimulation. I haven't heard anyone express confusion about the difference between sexual and nonsexual activities.

Regardless of any possible ambiguity, when Blumstein and Schwartz published their results and presented them in professional conferences, the term "lesbian bed death" was born.[3] That infamous term is with us today, twenty years later, even though we don't have current research to verify whether we're still at the bottom of the sexual frequency list. A lot has changed in that time—in research methodology, sex, and culture. So it would be excellent if a new study were done, so that we could ascertain whether lesbian couples still hold the low-frequency record.

But unfortunately, that isn't the case. All we can really do is look at research on other types of couples and get a sense of where we stand based on that information. Barry McCarthy, a psychologist and sex researcher with Washington University, estimates that about 15 percent of straight married couples have sex less than once a month.[4] In other words, 85 percent have sex once a month or more. Based on my experience, it's hard for me to imagine that 85 percent of the lesbian couples I know are having sex at least once a month, so my sense is that this commonly held belief—that women in long-term same-sex relationships have sex less frequently than other types of couples—is probably true.

That said, let me say one very important thing that will put all of this in perspective: *This is not a contest.* The question is not "How can we beat the straight couples in bed?" but "How can we have the kind of sex lives we want?"

If this last question resonates for you, take heart. Women who want to enrich their sex lives may be especially interested to know that my research shows that 20 percent of long-term lesbian lovers remain sexually active.[5] In 2007, I conducted an online survey of sexual patterns among women who partner with women. Of the 400 respondents, 187 had lived with a partner for at least two years. And among these 187 women, about 36 of them (20 percent) said they had sex twice a month or more; in other words, every week or two. For these sexually active (SA) women, sexual intimacy continues to be a vital and regular part of their ongoing relationship. When reading this and the other chapters, I want you to keep this sexually active (SA) subgroup in mind. It is a group I think a lot of women can—and would love to—join, and I believe this book can help.

"For women, sexual interest tends to decline with age."

Correlations between desire and age are often misguided or simply inaccurate, and I go into this in greater detail in chapter 6. The inaccuracy is highlighted in the results of a nationwide survey of adult sexual behavior conducted in 1994 by sociologist E. O. Laumann and colleagues from the University of Chicago.[6] In this study, a random sample of 1,749 American women ages 18–59 (of whom about 5 percent described themselves as "lesbian") were surveyed by experienced interviewers. About one-third of the women reported significant periods of having no interest in sex. When Laumann repeated this survey in 2005, using a sample of 13,882 women from 29 countries, he again found that about one-third of all the women reported significant periods of having no interest in sex.[7] Laumann described this group of women as having "low sexual desire."

So how old were the women in the "low sexual desire" group? This may be another surprise: 32 percent of the *youngest* women surveyed (ages 18–29), versus 27 percent of the oldest women (ages 50–59), fell into this category. This finding is very consistent with my clinical experience. The majority of women who have talked to me about a lack of sexual desire have been less than forty years old. Women over forty who complain about lack of desire frequently say, "I've always been that way." In other words, they weren't that interested in their twenties, either.

Ideas about hormones are closely linked to age, which is another explaination for the assumption that older women have less sexual interest. It is true that testosterone is linked to physical feelings of sexual desire, and that women experience a decrease in testosterone levels as they get older, often reporting a corresponding decrease in the intensity of sexual sensations. However, the impact of this decrease has been highly overrated. Even some younger women attribute their lack of sexual interest to "low testosterone," implying that they have no conscious control over the situation. And some older women say they enjoy sex even more than when they were younger, as they've learned more about their sexual likes and dislikes.

Perhaps we need a broader definition of desire. To most women, sexual desire means more than just biological, genital–sexual urges. Many women want sexual intimacy because they like the physical closeness, the emotional connection, and the good feelings that come up after they begin a sexual experience. Older women have often had more sexual experiences to validate this connection between sexual and emotional intimacy. Because they have lived through these experiences, they know how sexual contact can bring partners closer and its absence can widen a chasm between them. For these women, "sexual desire" includes the desire to repeat an experience that has been powerfully reinforcing in both physical and emotional ways. Their broader perspective of desire may override the biological impact of hormonal fluctuations.

Another important thing to take into consideration is the probability that there is confusion between "age" and "relationship duration." It is evident that sexual frequency decreases over time with the same partner, and obviously, older women have had more time to develop relationships of longer duration. Is a lack of sexual desire reported by a fifty-year-old related to her age or to the fact that she's been with her partner for twenty years? It's just too simplistic to say it's all about age and hormones.

"Single women experience more sexual desire than women in relationships."

While it's true that desire seems to decrease as relationship duration increases, in both of the Laumann studies mentioned above, more single women reported a lack of sexual desire than did women in stable, long-term relationships. This contradicts the belief that single women, presumably not having much or any sex, would be more filled with desire than a partnered woman. That belief is based on the "biological urge" model. Hunger is a biological urge. If you don't satisfy hunger, it gets stronger; if you don't satisfy sexual desire, it gets stronger. That's a perfectly logical explanation—if you think desire is mostly biological.

But there's little evidence that female desire is a biological urge. In fact, for women, the adage "use it or lose it" is more apt. Women who have regular access to the same sexual partner have more opportunities to "use it." They are more likely to receive positive reinforcement on a regular basis, which makes them more likely to want sex more.

"Sexual abuse during childhood leads to low desire in adult women."

Research evidence does not indicate that abuse causes a lack of sexual desire, and I go into more detail about this in chapter 5. Research conducted by Cindy Meston, from the University of Texas, and Julia Heimann, the director of the Kinsey Sex Research Institute, shows no clear evidence of a simple link between sexual abuse and decreased desire. Their study did show, however, that women who were sexually abused as children are more likely to engage in sexually risky behavior, such as having multiple partners, not protecting themselves from danger, or having hostile and anxious feelings during sex.[8]

Unfortunately, many people—including therapists and their clients—have assumed a simple link between lack of sexual desire and childhood sexual abuse. This is what leads some women to say, "I wonder if something happened that I can't remember, because I have no desire." This statement puts these women in a very helpless position. How can you work on something you can't remember? While women who experienced sexual trauma need support for working through it, it is a mistake to assume it is the cause of a lack of sexual desire. There's no research data to support this idea, and it can, in fact, be a deterrent to working out other sexual concerns with a partner.

It is also important to know that same-sex orientation is not "caused" by a traumatic event such as sexual abuse. After all, the vast majority of women who have been sexually abused are heterosexual. Even though most people know this intellectually, there are a number of statements which convey a different feeling: "She's not really lesbian; she's afraid of men because of what happened to her." "She's looking for safety, not sex." "She really wants a mother, not a lover."

These kinds of statements are all based on psychological interpretations that can go both ways. Maybe straight women really want a father instead of a lover, or want safety more than sex, or are afraid of men. No matter which way they're directed, such statements are unverifiable, unhelpful, disempowering, and terribly simplistic.

The impact of sexual abuse is rarely simple. It is usually complex and depends on many variables, including the relationship with the abuser, parental reactions to the abuse, and the degree of emotional support available for the victim. Based on these factors, a woman who has experienced abuse may feel either helpless and isolated by her trauma, or empowered and able to connect with a sexual partner.

"The frequency of sex is not really important to most partnered lesbians."

Based on my professional experience and personal research, this seems completely false. In my 2007 online survey, 90 percent of the respondents said they thought regular sexual contact was important in a long-term relationship.[9] When asked what they considered "regular," most women said they meant "every week or two." In many conversations with many women, what I've heard is that sex is very important to them—even though they are often frustrated or disappointed about it. Couples who have gone for years without any sexual intimacy will often say that they feel frustrated, or inadequate, or pressured, or guilty about this issue. Sex is clearly important, even if it's not happening.

Sex therapist Barry McCarthy points out that sexual frustration can become the main focus for a troubled relationship. His research is done with heterosexual couples but seems pertinent for all of us. What he points out is that happily married couples are usually happy about their sex life but say that sex is only moderately important to their overall satisfaction. However, when couples are unhappy, sex can become the primary focus of their discontent—and the reason to leave a relationship.[10]

I've really noticed this in my work. Very often, when I've asked women why they ended a relationship, the first thing they bring up is sexual frustration—a lack of sex, to be specific. And even though we may think "quantity is not quality," the numbers are what people talk about: once a month, or once a year, or zero times in the past two years. I rarely hear complaints about the quality of sex when it happens—it just doesn't happen enough. And based on my experience, that seems very important to many women.

"Once nonsexual relationship problems
are resolved, sexual attraction returns."

It's obvious that many couples who aren't having sexual intimacy with each other are also distressed about other issues; conflicts about money, housework, and family abound. And of course it's hard to work on sexual intimacy with someone you're fighting with. Often it's the decrease in sexual intimacy that finally motivates couples to go to counseling so that they can resolve their fights and conflicts. Very often, therapists and clients hope that resolving nonsexual concerns will lead to a spontaneous resurrection of sexual feelings with each other.

Usually, this doesn't happen. Therapist David Treadway refers to this as the "dirty little secret" of couple's therapy: It doesn't seem to help with sexual issues, even when it helps with everything else. After therapy, couples often report reduced conflict, improved communication, and greater intimacy in many ways . . . but not sexually.[11]

It appears that couples who want to improve their sex lives need to talk specifically about sex. They may have to wait until their communication has improved and they've reconnected with positive feelings for each other, but at some point they need to talk about what happened with their sexual relationship and what would make it better for both of them. Hoping for spontaneous remission is unrealistic.

So does this recommend going to one therapist for couple's counseling and to another for specific sexual issues? That depends on several factors. If you're having a specific sexual problem, such as the inability to have an orgasm, or painful sex, you might benefit most from a sex therapist. If your concern is a more general lack of desire, or a discrepancy in desire between you and your partner, your general couple's therapist may help—under certain conditions. Are you comfortable talking about sex with your therapist?

Does your therapist seem comfortable talking with you about it? Can you both be graphic if you need to be? Would you feel more comfortable getting specific with someone who doesn't know you as well as your current therapist? The important thing is to try to talk about it and see how you feel afterward. And if you don't feel good about it, try someone else.

If you want to try talking with a sex therapist, the website for the American Association of Sex Educators, Counselors, and Therapists provides a list of people in your area: www.aasect.org.

MOST OF THE statements covered in this chapter have to do with what is seen as "normal" and "common." And as I said at the beginning of this chapter, knowing the answer to the question "Am I normal?" is valuable. But it's not enough. Feeling normal reduces stigma and helps us feel supported, but that doesn't mean we can't hope for more, and we certainly should not rely on standards of normalcy to conduct our personal lives. If you or your partner responds to sexual concerns by saying, "This is normal," take some time to stop and consider these questions: "How do I feel about this?" "How important is sexual intimacy to me?" "Is this good for me and for us?"

This is a very important point. Taken the wrong way, facts about what's "normal" can lead us to resign ourselves to an unfulfilling situation. *What if I leave her and everything we have together, and then just go through this all over again with someone else? Or, If it's so normal, maybe I should just accept what I have and try to live with it.* These are rationalizations for unhappiness. These are reasons to settle for less.

The problem with "normal" is not just that it's shortsighted. Relying on common perspectives of normalcy clouds your decision-making abilities. Besides, many things that are very normal and common aren't good for us. For example, in the United States, it's common to watch hours of television, to be sedentary, to eat poorly, and to dislike your job. Few of us think these are good things.

In fact, if normalcy were the gold standard, we wouldn't be in same-sex relationships at all—we'd be straight, like the vast majority of women.

2

Spontaneous vs. Responsive Desire

THE GERMANS CALL it *Verliebtheit*. In Denmark, it's *forelskelse*. In Brazil they sing songs about *paixonite;* in Russia, влюблённость (vlyu-*blyon*-nost). In Spanish, it's *enamoramiento,* but in Catalan, it's *enamorament*. Strangely, there's no colloquial word for it in English, so the translation is clunky, but what I'm talking about here is "the state of falling in love." Psychologist Dorothy Tennov refers to it as "limerence," defined as "an involuntary cognitive and emotional state, with continuous, intrusive thoughts and intense longing for the other."[1]

New lovers—that is, people experiencing limerence—lock their doors. They turn off all communication devices, ignore daily duties, and spend countless hours in bed. They function without sleep and often with little food. They feel as if they could almost walk on water. And there's a sense of expansion that feels literal, physical: "My heart feels so full." "I feel like I could burst." "I'm on Cloud Nine." "This is something bigger than me." In many instances, limerence leads to distorted thinking patterns, a kind of "limerence logic," in which the intensity of one's feelings is proof that this is True Love, so it's easy to justify risky decisions—after all, "it was meant to be," right? We all need to be a little careful with limerence, keeping one foot on the ground and remembering the mind-bending power of this transient state.

But for the most part, limerence is a wonderful, romantic frame of mind that makes a woman lean in toward her partner, pay her a lot of attention, think about her all the time, and fantasize about making love with her. Sexual energy explodes during this phase. All of it feels just like an amphetamine high.

There are reasons for this! Cool scientific analysis of hot passion reveals at least four distinct factors that contribute to the bliss of new love.

① Biochemical reactions, which produce powerful feelings that seem beyond our control.

② Behavioral changes, which build anticipation for sexual excitement.

③ Anxiety, which can intensify sexual feelings.

④ Obstacles and adversity, which only make the feelings stronger—and there are often plenty of obstacles and adversity in any new lesbian relationship

THOUGH THE ENTIRE experience of limerence feels completely spontaneous and inspired, with closer examination of these four factors, it's very easy to see a completely determined sequence of events that leads up to, and results in, a very *predictable* flood of desire.

Did I just burst your bubble? If you think that's disappointing, think again. This is actually very good news! If you know which factors channel into hot sexual feelings, you'll also know what it takes to recreate those feelings when the initial flood of passion subsides.

Like it or not, spontaneous desire, if it ever does exist between two people, fades after a few months (or weeks or years), and that is a loss. But it's replaced by something wonderful and sustainable. Before I go into that, let's first take a closer look at those four factors, which act as undercurrents, propelling those initial feelings that seem so spontaneous and blissful.

The Biochemistry Factor

In her fascinating book *Why We Love,* anthropologist Helen Fisher describes her studies of brain activity in men and women who had recently fallen in love.[2] She and her colleagues used functional magnetic resonance imaging (fMRI) technology to identify which regions in the brain are activated during periods of romantic bliss. They found that falling in love is associated with changes in baseline levels of three neurotransmitters: dopamine, norepinephrine, and serotonin. This biochemical triad, Fisher suggests, creates the "high" of falling in love. Each one of them plays a specific role, shaping emotions, thoughts, and physiological arousal in the early stages of a romantic relationship.

Elevated dopamine levels can increase attention, motivation, and goal-directed behaviors, and they are also associated with novel stimuli. New lovers have a one-track mind. They think about each other all the time; they only want to be together; they exclude other people and other activities. When people say they feel "addicted to love," they're not mistaken. Increased dopamine is associated with the dependency and craving that characterize all kinds of addictions. It's also associated with a pounding heart and accelerated breathing—physical reactions that accompany feelings of ecstasy and bliss but can easily channel into anxiety or fear if something seems to be threatening the relationship. Given how intense the craving is, it isn't surprising that a perceived threat can lead to frantic efforts to reconnect and an intensified focus on the loved one. That's what dopamine can do in a new love affair.

Norepinephrine is derived from dopamine and also produces feelings of exhilaration, sleeplessness, excessive energy, and loss of appetite. It leads to making love all night, feeling gloriously optimistic, running on no food or rest. Some people take illicit drugs to produce these feelings. Others fall in love. The smallest details of special moments together are remembered clearly, because norepinephrine also seems to help with memory for new stimuli.

Serotonin levels seem to be *lower* for new lovers, and Fisher suggests that this explains the obsessive thinking that goes on when people fall in love. Clinical research has shown that lower levels of serotonin are associated with "ruminations," the incessant, irresistible, repetitive thoughts that we call "obsessions." (Because of this, SSRIs—that is, selective serotonin reuptake inhibitors—are routinely prescribed to people experiencing depression, anxiety, and/or obsessive–compulsive disorder, as these drugs increase serotonin levels and thereby decrease repetitive negative thoughts and obsessive symptoms.) Sentiments such as "I can't stop thinking about you" and "You're always on my mind" could actually be low serotonin levels at work.

Other researchers suggest that testosterone is also at work when you're falling in love, part of a powerful, self-perpetuating loop: Testosterone fuels desire for sexual activity, and sexual activity increases testosterone levels.[3] New lovers make love with each other more, fantasize about sex more, masturbate more. Feelings of aggressiveness accompany testosterone, leading to more goal-oriented, assertive behavior. And usually, the goal is . . . guess what? More sex!

There are different hypotheses about oxytocin, the "bonding chemical" released during warm physical experiences like breast-feeding and orgasm. Those wonderful feelings of warmth and gratitude could be an oxytocin flood, which could certainly explain the "afterglow" of a good sexual experience. Women release much more oxytocin than men, and some suggest this is why we are so quick to develop feelings of long-term attachment.[4] Whether it's true or not, there's certainly a commonly held belief that women want emotional commitment more than men do. Perhaps the disparate levels of oxytocin contribute to that difference. When two women get together, there's all that oxytocin, blending blissful attachment with sexual excitement. Maybe this explains the intense merging lovers feel when they say, "I'm yours." That's probably oxytocin sealing the deal.

The Behavioral Factor

New lovers plan their sexual encounters well in advance, in great detail, and with excited anticipation. They choose flattering clothes to wear, romantic restaurants with dim lights, music with a subtle and sexual beat, activities that allow plenty of touching, and conversations that promote intimacy. They communicate a great deal of interest, both subtly and directly, and make themselves available for a sexual response. Their behaviors constitute an expanded form of foreplay, building desire for sexual contact.

You know what it's like to try to impress someone. The effort brings out the best in you. You accentuate your most positive qualities and try to hide or minimize your less appealing ones. You take better care of yourself so that you'll look and feel better to someone else. You practice your best communication skills, listening attentively and talking candidly. You whisper sweet nothings to each other, expressing love and admiration . . . and you get to hear how someone else loves and admires *you*. You are very active, planning interesting and fun things to do together. You treat the other person in ways that feel loving, tender, and protective . . . and then you get immediate, positive reinforcement. You enjoy seeing the results of your own effort to shine, and you love hearing the positive feedback all this good behavior generates.

Now, you may think you're doing all this only to impress her, but really, you're impressing yourself too. Hearing someone's love and admiration is quite an ego boost, but it's your *own* behavior that really increases your self-esteem. Martin Seligman, one of the most influential psychologists of the century, writes extensively about self-esteem. His major point is that self-esteem comes from *doing* positive behaviors.[5]

What do you do for a new lover? Cook dinner for her, pick up her dry cleaning, help plan her work presentation, buy gifts for her, look for ways to make her feel good. Doing nice things for her enhances your positive feelings about yourself. It may seem as if you're thrilled by how much she appreciates you, but actually, you're thrilled about how much you are appreciating yourself—the phrase "I love the way I am when I'm with you" comes to mind. And there's a self-congratulatory element that adds to the ego boost: "I'm so happy to know I can feel this way again!" "I've still got it!" "I feel so young again!" You feel so pleased to know you're capable of having such wonderful, powerful feelings. You may also end up feeling a little smug about being a great lover, because your partner is so sexually responsive to you. Congratulating yourself reinforces a positive, expanded sense of self-esteem and adds to the wonderful sense of savoring the experience with your partner.

Most of us have noticed that it's easier to pursue someone sexually if you're feeling good about yourself; and then, positive sexual experiences make you feel even better. This is confirmed by research, which shows a positive correlation between sexual feelings and self-esteem.[6] Conversely, sexual dissatisfaction is highly associated with low self-esteem, so feeling bad about yourself makes you less likely to want to be sexual. While it's not clear which comes first, there's definitely a cycle of reinforcement that's going on.

The main point of all this? That there is *nothing spontaneous* about all the careful planning that goes into early passion. These are foreplay behaviors, and they are very effective in creating feelings of sexual desire.

The Anxiety Factor

We don't usually think of anxiety as a good thing, but a certain amount of it does seem to intensify passionate feelings. So no wonder the beginning of a new love relationship is so powerful. There is so much of fodder for angst! "Does she like me as much as I like her?" "Am I going to make an idiot out of myself?" "Will she call me again?" "Can this work out?" You may think the anxiety is there "in spite of" the passion, but actually, it's probably adding to it.

A classic social psychology experiment demonstrated that anxiety tends to increase sexual desire.[7] College students were asked to cross a bridge that was carefully designed to look frightening and to make them feel very anxious. They were met on the other side by an attractive young woman, who was actually role-playing as part of the experiment. A control group of students also met the same young woman, but they did not have to cross the frightening bridge and therefore were not in a heightened state of anxiety. Afterward, both groups of students were asked to rate how anxious they had been *and* how attracted they felt to the woman. As predicted, the students who had to cross the scary bridge were more anxious— and more attracted to her—than the students who took a much safer route.

Most people have noticed that they become more anxious in a new love relationship. What they don't realize is that anxiety itself increases intensity by adding a biochemical charge to your feelings of passion. A colleague of mine, a psychology professor, had an *Aha!* moment reading about the "dangerous bridge" study. When she was younger, she went on a group rafting trip on a difficult river. There was a serious accident, and several people were hurt. The professor was chosen to get help. She approached someone in the parking lot who gave her a ride back to the rafting center. On the ride, she noticed that she felt incredibly attracted to the driver. She was breathing quickly, her heart was pounding, and she felt tingling in her fingers and toes. All the way back to the center, she fantasized about kissing and fondling the driver. She also felt mystified and peculiar about her intense reaction.

After reading the study, the professor's reaction made sense to her. And biochemically, it all adds up: Acute stress produces an adrenaline rush, which in turn activates a state of arousal—the so-called "fight or flight response." Most people know this. But what many don't know is that after the impending danger is gone, the arousal can linger and can be interpreted in other ways . . . such as sexual attraction. For my colleague, the acute stress of the rafting accident set off physiological reactions that lingered after she was out of danger and that were then focused on the driver.

This is important to keep in mind, because anxiety can actually come in handy when it comes to sustaining intimacy. Our automatic response to anxiety is usually to try to make it go away by avoiding it, ignoring it, or neutralizing it. In fact, that response is so automatic, you may not realize you're doing it. In a relationship, many of us avoid feelings of anxiety through denial; by avoiding talking about anything threatening, sensitive, or potentially conflictual. That does keep anxiety at bay—but it also keeps other feelings at bay too.

Avoiding conflict helps people feel safe, but a total lack of conflict also leads to complacency and boredom. By deciding to tolerate some anxiety in our relationship, we are able to deal with threatening or sensitive issues and conflicts directly. The fact that the adrenaline charge from facing your issues can actually be channeled into sexual excitement is just icing on the cake!

The Obstacles and Adversity Factor

In his book, *The Erotic Mind*, the sexologist Jack Morin suggests that adversity is an essential component of sexual attraction: No obstacles = no excitement.[8] Obstacles may be internal or external . . . and there are often plenty of both for lesbian lovers. Internal obstacles include fears about being lesbian, being rejected, or being trapped. External obstacles can involve falling for someone who isn't available or who lives across the country, or the lack of acceptance of same-sex relationships. And it's not hard to see how societal disapproval contributes to an "us against the world" attitude that in turn can intensify one's attachment to her partner. Disapproval from family or friends can have the same effect (much to the chagrin of those who try to pull the couple apart because they are "trying to help"). According to Morin, these kinds of obstacles just fuel the flames of passion.

One response to adversity is to join forces and face it together; another is to back away quietly. Psychologist K. L. Falco suggests that gay people constrict themselves by constant hypervigilance, censorship, and nondisclosure.[9] Because we're busy protecting ourselves from perceived threats in the environment, we feel less free to be ourselves, to be open with our same-sex lovers, to claim our sexuality. There's plenty of adversity out there when you love other women. Facing it directly can increase your sexual desire, but backing away probably suppresses it. That's a choice that most of us make almost every day, usually without awareness. But what if we were aware? Might we feel more sexual if we confronted anti-sexual bias more directly? Do women touch each other in public because they feel more desire for each other—or do they feel more desire because they touch each other in public? Wouldn't that be interesting to notice?

ALAS, THE ROMANTIC and sexual intensity of a new relationship can't go on forever. And so, like it or not, we all eventually revert to baseline levels of biochemicals and behaviors. That's inevitable and probably fortunate. The body can't keep churning out all those luscious biochemicals. We'd be worn out! And we can't spend all that time being charming and attentive when we have to run our jobs and households and the rest of life.

So what, then?

Well, sometimes we "wake up" from limerence to realize that there isn't enough substance underlying the initial attraction and that we don't want to continue the relationship. If that's not the case—if we *do* want to have a deeper, lasting sexual intimacy with this person, then we have to let go of some romantic fantasies and embrace some realistic changes. When sex stops feeling easy and spontaneous, partners can interpret the changes in ways that set the stage for chronic, nonproductive cycles of conflict and avoidance. One misses the magic and the other assumes the inevitable. Between these opposite poles, neither partner has a realistic grasp of what nourishes sexuality in long-term relationships. Nor are they realistic about the long-term risks of drifting into an asexual relationship.

If, as is often the case, there is one partner with less sexual interest, she may feel relieved, thinking, *At last, we can settle into sane, comfortable sharing of our lives.* For her, the change is expected and simply means it's time to focus on other things that are equally or more important than sex. The other partner, however, may feel disappointed and wonder whether something has gone wrong. This is when some troubling questions might arise, such as, *If I no longer feel very attracted to her, does that mean she's not right for me?* Or *If I don't feel an urge to make love, does that mean there's a problem with me—or with the relationship?* Or *If my sexual responses become less intense, does that mean sex isn't important to me anymore?*

For help with these realistic changes, we can turn to Rosemary Basson, MD, also known as "the new guru of female sexuality."[10] Dr. Basson is a professor in the departments of Psychiatry and Obstetrics and Gynecology at the University of British Columbia. She suggests that we need a new model for female sexual desire, one that fits the reality of most women's sexual experiences. She calls this the "responsive desire" model.

The conventional viewpoint, Dr. Basson points out, is based on a male model of the sex drive, which is based on hormones and genital stirrings—or what we might label "spontaneous" urges to have sex. But most women don't feel sexually driven in that way. In fact, 30 to 40 percent of all women express concern about low sexual desire, labeling themselves as "abnormal" or "sexually dysfunctional."[11] Furthermore, a majority of sexually satisfied women also say they don't feel much spontaneous desire. What they *do* feel is the ability to generate desire by intentionally seeking erotic stimuli, which in turn elicit a sexual response. In other words, the "response" in responsive desire is first felt by you, and later by your partner. This is wonderful news. Instead of waiting passively for spontaneous desire to strike, it's entirely possible to actively set the stage in which sexual desire and arousal can flourish.

Dr. Basson states what most of us know from experience: Sex for women often starts with a conscious decision, not a hormonal or genital drive. We may decide to have sex because we want the emotional intimacy or because we want to please a partner. Women are less likely than men to seek sex for genital tension relief, and are more likely to seek other emotional rewards that often accompany sex. Furthermore, we're less likely than men to feel driven by spontaneous biological urges. We may joke about which part of the body is leading the charge, but in reality, for us, it's usually the brain.

The physiological responses of arousal, such as lubrication and clitoral engorgement, often happen *after* sexual contact begins. As many women say, "Once we get started, it feels great!" According to Dr. Basson, the reason it feels great once you've gotten started is that you begin deliberately focusing on sexual stimuli—erotic thoughts, fantasies, pleasurable sensations—and this causes physiological arousal, which feels good, so you want to continue sexual activity. Then your own erotic thoughts, as well as your partner's physical stimulation, combine to heighten your arousal. And this is how sexual energy travels from your brain down your body, into your pelvis, where it usually culminates in the ultimate physical pleasure of orgasm. The energy doesn't come from some underground wellspring of sexual desire. It comes from your intentional choices, is enhanced by your thoughts, and then merges with your body to produce a lovely experience.

What are the implications of this model for female sexual desire? For one thing, it's empowering! You can be a very sexually active person, even if you've never had a spontaneous urge in your life. Responsive desire creates an intimate loop between lovers. You decide to try to get yourself turned on so that you can enjoy having emotional and sexual contact with your partner. You pay more attention to yourself, to the sensations and thoughts that are arousing to you. Your partner does the same. You begin to feel more turned on, and you see your partner getting turned on also. This increases arousal for both of you. And so it goes. What starts as a self-centered focus on your own sensual pleasure magnifies pleasure for both of you, and leads to feeling more connected emotionally and sexually. It's a magical loop. You create your own desire, which helps create your partner's, and she does the same for you.

This model is also very normalizing. If you don't have spontaneous urges, welcome to the club: At least a third of other women don't either.[12] And it's inspiring to know that intentionality trumps spontaneity in the long-run. Intentionality is the way to sustain sexual intimacy in a long-term relationship.

There's one question that always comes up when I talk with women about how to intentionally create sexual desire: "If it doesn't come naturally, why should I have to work at it?"

The obvious reason is that if you wait for sexual feelings to come up naturally, they may not come up at all. Spontaneous desire just doesn't seem to be the way it works for most women— especially after the limerence phase. For many women, the choice is between intentional sex or no sex at all. So unless you're ready for a life without sex, it's in your best interest to learn how to make it happen. And the research on marital and sexual satisfaction suggests that you'll be happier with your partner if you sustain sexual intimacy with her. You may even enjoy knowing you took charge of your sexual feelings, instead of floating along waiting to catch a fast current.

The other reason to cultivate responsive desire is that you want your relationship to last. An asexual relationship is fertile turf for attraction to somebody else. I've heard dozens of women say they left a primary relationship because they wanted to have sex again.

Often they say something like, "I already had plenty of friends. I wanted a sexual partner." Then, when they feel the "spontaneous" desire with a new person, they think, *She must be the right one for me.* Their contrast has been between "spontaneous desire" and "no desire at all." There's been no solid middle ground of sustained sexuality to glue the relationship together.

Our cultural training makes us resistant to being intentional about sex. Planning for sex goes against the grain of everything we learned as women about sexuality and leaves us vulnerable to feelings of guilt and shame. The guilt about deliberately trying to get ourselves turned on is similar to guilt about masturbation. We're supposed to respond to someone else, not to our own "dirty" thoughts and images. It's okay to be swept away on waves of romantic passion, but it's not okay to deliberately generate the currents. Many women think they should only focus on a partner during sex and feel guilty about using sexual fantasies to help them get aroused or reach orgasm. Other women just feel guilty thinking about sex at all. All those years of guarding our "privates," not naming our body parts correctly, or simply not talking about sex can culminate in a giant case of guilt when sex is on the brain. And finally, sex is about pleasure, and our Puritan work ethic doesn't encourage us to sit around thinking about pleasure. The deliberate behaviors and thoughts that go into being intentional about sex and creating responsive desire are in direct opposition to most female sexual indoctrination.

Being intentional about sex also makes you vulnerable to feelings of shame, because it means acknowledging that you want it. There's nothing like extending a hand and getting slapped away.

It feels humiliating and can make you wish you hadn't reached out at all. Our interpretations of sexual rejection are rife with shameful themes. *She doesn't want me because I'm not attractive,* or *because I'm not a good lover,* or *because she wants someone else.* These are all thoughts that can cut to the core of self-esteem. It's much safer to pretend that sex might "just happen" than it is to step out on a limb, express your intention, and hope for the best.

Of course, there can also be a big self-esteem boost that comes from doing exactly that. You may be vulnerable to feelings of shame but also recognize the courage you have in being intentional about sex. You're validating your sexuality and your partner's, and that's a good feeling—even if you don't get what you want.

A friend of mine offered another explanation of why we resist being intentional about sex. "Laziness," she said. This friend is a hard worker. She works long hours, keeps a spotless household, and bikes and runs long distances by herself and with her partner. She also enjoys a rich sex life with her partner and attributes this to shared values and effort. In her perspective, people long for effortless sex—but to her, anything worth having is worth making the effort for. It would be like hoping to have great biceps without ever lifting any weights or great thighs without leaving the sofa. And of course laziness can be self-perpetuating: Being lazy results in doing less, which makes you feel more lazy. The "laziness" hypothesis sounds a bit harsh, but my friend's attitude has clearly worked for her.

A close corollary to laziness is entitlement, the sense that things should come easily to me, just because I'm me. If sexual desire isn't happening, there must be something wrong with someone else—not me. Maybe the relationship isn't good enough, or my partner isn't attractive enough, or life isn't treating me well enough to keep me feeling sexually vibrant. The idea that I should *do something* to generate feelings of desire for myself and my partner can be deeply offensive, almost like acknowledging some inadequacy. Far better to dwell on fantasies about the perfect partner who would engender my lust than to humbly accept my lack of desire and try to do something about it.

So is there a way to tell, at the beginning of a relationship, if it has the potential to sustain sexual intimacy? Not to be a wet blanket, but a lot depends on how realistic both of you can be about sexual desire. If you both believe sex should happen spontaneously and effortlessly, you're doomed. Those intoxicating conversations about magic, chemistry, or divine intervention? Enjoy them, but don't take them too seriously. What you need to know is if the intentional mind can step in when limerence fades.

Not to be a really wet blanket, but let me also point out the importance of listening carefully to what people tell you about themselves. If someone tells you her previous sexual relationships faded within a few months, or that she felt "pressured" by her ex, take heed. Likewise, if she implies that her sexual feelings are dictated by hormones, beware. It's one thing to acknowledge that "I feel more turned on a few days before my period"—lots of women do—but is that the only time she wants to have sex? And how does she react to the idea of planning time for sex? If she says, "That's too awkward," chances are she's not going to appreciate the nuances of responsive desire. And if she complains that you expect too much sexually, take a big pause. "Expectation" has a pejorative connotation, implying that you're being set up as a controller to rebel against. You could find yourself scheduling time for sexual intimacy, only to be told your expectations are a turn-off.

Never fear, there *are* women who love the expectation of being sexual and look forward to it with anticipation. They think about sex as a team effort and talk about how "we can do this together." They know that early-stage passion is easy, but that it takes a partnership to sustain sexuality over the long haul. These women are realistic about the challenges of making time and space for sex, and they can laugh about how hard it is to get turned on in the middle of daily life's demands. They do not take it personally when you're not in the mood, because they understand that we have to start with turning ourselves on first.

So while you're feeling the bliss of new passion, try to engage your brain enough to assess your long-term possibilities. Sex really is a team sport, and both players need to participate for the play to happen. Hopefully, you and your partner place a similar value on sexual intimacy. If you think sexual intimacy is the core experience that glues a couple together, and she thinks it's nice when you have time for it, I predict you'll have problems. Your chances for cultivating responsive desire are going to be slimmer if the basic value isn't there.

Most sex therapists decry the "myth of spontaneity." But is it a myth? The research certainly suggests that falling in love sets off torrents of biochemicals that produce feelings of pleasure, focus, excitement, and bonding. To some extent, those feelings are beyond conscious control and therefore could be called "spontaneous." But when we look at what new lovers *do* when they first start a sexual relationship, it's clear that a great deal of careful planning goes into setting the stage for sexual intimacy. In other words, much of that "spontaneity" is created intentionally.

This intention is what gives us hope, and this is what I discuss in further detail in chapter 10.

Biochemical rushes have to settle down eventually, but intentionality is with us forever, and the behaviors associated with limerence can be recreated to powerful effect. In chapters 9 through 12, you'll find an in-depth discussion of how to take charge of your sexuality and how to generate responsive desire—the kind that lasts.

common
stumbling blocks
to intimacy

3

The Dynamics of Desire Discrepancy

THIS IS SOMETHING I hear very often in my sexual intimacy workshops: "I must have a really low sex drive. I've wondered what's wrong with me. Did something happen to me? I don't know what it is, but I just don't think about sex. If it were up to me, I'd be fine with no sex. But she pressures me, so I have to work at it. Then it isn't spontaneous anyway, so that doesn't feel right either."

And then there's the other end of the spectrum: "I still love her, and I want us to stay together . . . but I don't want to just give up on sex. Do I change my expectations or my partner?"

These comments reflect the two sides of the most prevalent and persistent problem in lesbian sexual relationships: One partner wants sex much more than the other. The clinical term for this phenomenon is "desire discrepancy." It usually manifests after the honeymoon high subsides and women return to their baseline levels of sexual interest.

"Desire discrepancy" is a great term because it takes the onus off either individual and redirects attention to the *real* source of the problem, which is that the women involved simply have different degrees of interest in sex. One is not more "mentally healthy" or "spiritually evolved" than the other. They're just different.

Yet all too often, desire discrepancy turns into a difficult and prolonged conflict. For many couples, the first stage involves intense, repetitive arguments in which each person assumes her position as being "higher" or "lower" on the sexual-desire continuum. Each position carries certain emotions and perceptions that tend to perpetuate it.

The partner who wants more initiates the most sexual contact and therefore gets "rejected" the most. This is hard on her self-esteem, and she may find herself thinking, *I'm not attractive enough. She's not in love with me. She'd be more interested in sex with someone else.* Once her self-esteem drops as a result of these perceived rejections, she becomes even more emotionally fragile and open to more perceptions of rejection. After a while, this usually leads not just to hurt feelings but also to anger and resentment. She may feel as if she has to do all the relationship work. She may begin to make negative psychological interpretations about her partner, thinking, rightly or wrongly, that her partner has some deep-seated problems about sex. She may even challenge her partner's "lesbianness."

The partner with less desire also has intense negative feelings that can shift over time. At the beginning, she may feel guilty, wondering, *Should I tell her I'm just not attracted to her? I don't want to hurt her feelings.* She may try to avoid hurting her partner's feelings, saying, "It's not you, it's me." Internally, she might tell herself the problem is that she's not in love, or she's still in love with an ex, or she has unresolved "sexual issues." All of this internal analysis usually results in sexual paralysis, and the stalemate goes on.

At this point, both partners are negatively interpreting neutral events. Lack of sexual desire isn't necessarily a reflection on anyone. The fact is that everyone's desire drops after the honeymoon, and in order to bring it back up, most women have to make a conscious effort. So instead of thinking, *She's not attracted to me anymore,* it's more helpful to think, *How can I help her stir up some sexual feelings?*

Instead of taking this positive approach, however, most couples get into debates about who's controlling whom. It's true that the partner with less desire often feel pressured, but the reality is that she usually sets the tone for the sexual relationship. It takes two people to have a happy sexual encounter, and if one isn't happy, the other won't be either. There's no such thing as sexual intimacy that's great for one person and not the other. Reluctant participation isn't very satisfying for either partner, and that's why women with higher desire usually complain that they feel controlled.

Women who have lower desire have a hard time with the idea that they're controlling the relationship. Look at it this way: If "high desire" wants sex every other week, that would be twenty-six times per year. If "low desire" never wants sex, that would be zero times per year. Who's getting more of what she wants? I'm guessing the balance tips toward "low desire."

There's another factor that contributes to the person with higher desire feeling controlled: *intermittent reinforcement.* From studies of learning theory, we know that it is hardest to give up a behavior if you get occasional, unpredictable reinforcement. This is because you know that there is a reward sometimes, but you never know exactly when, so you keep trying, in case *this* is the magic time. Parents and pet owners know this. If you occasionally and unpredictably give your child or your pet a treat, they will keep asking just in case *this* is the time you're going to say yes again. When the person with low desire "gives in" from time to time, the person with high desire gets "trained" to think that initiating a lot will yield some success. She may even joke about "wearing her down," but what's actually wearing down is the supply of good feelings between the two partners. Occasional "success" doesn't override the build-up of resentment that comes from feeling at the mercy of your partner's whims.

At some point, the lower-desire partner says something like, "You don't give me a chance to want you." She may say she'll take a step forward if the other takes a step back. Then the higher-desire partner calls her bluff and stops initiating sex. This seemingly commonsense solution usually backfires. It may be how it works in dancing, but it doesn't seem to work in sexual relationships. Instead, nothing sexual happens. Both partners stay locked in their frustrating roles. Eventually, they give up the struggle and begin a long slow process of disengaging.

Disengaging involves avoidance, and this is something women know a lot about—we've had a lot of training. We don't learn much about how to initiate sexual contact, but we sure can ward it off. Our culture provides us with plenty of examples of straight couples in which women have low desire and are very crafty at avoiding sexual advances from their partners. Anyone who wants to avoid sex has plenty of standard methods to choose from: headaches, other plans, leaving the scene, etc. One woman in a workshop said she couldn't have sex on weekend mornings—the only time she and her partner had privacy—because she had to do the weekly grocery shopping. Another explained that tennis practice took up all her free time. A third needed to mow the lawn before it got too hot or rained.

In my sexual intimacy workshops, I usually ask women to identify some of the ways they have learned to avoid opportunities for sexual contact. Everyone laughs, and no one has any trouble with this question. Here are some of the answers:

- Going to bed early because you're too tired.
- Going to bed late because you're not sleepy yet.
- Jumping out of bed on weekends to go grocery shopping.
- Getting on the computer or the telephone.
- Scheduling so many social activities that there's no private time left over.
- Forgetting to take a shower before getting in bed together.
- Starting an argument just before you have some private time together.
- Watching television in bed.

The big problem with avoidance is that it works so well. Avoidance keeps anxiety at bay, so we don't have to confront the problem. But instead of being a solution, avoidance actually *perpetuates* the problem. If you never face challenges, you don't give yourself a chance to learn that you can handle them. Instead, sexual problems become more intractable the longer they continue. As time passes, you feel more awkward and self-conscious about sex, more anxious, and more inclined to avoid sexual situations. Allowing this to continue sets the stage for a crisis to end the relationship.

Shelley first contacted me for information about one of my intimacy workshops for lesbian couples. She wanted to attend with her partner, Jan. But I didn't hear from her again until she called a year later. Now, sitting tearfully in my office, she told me she and Jan had separated, and as we talked, I quickly realized that desire discrepancy was the primary cause of their breakup. "Except for sex," Shelley said, "things were good. I loved her, and we had a great life together."

The two women had met when Shelley was thirty. During their twelve years together, Shelley felt a great deal of love and companionship with Jan. However, she had wanted more sexual intimacy with Jan for a long time. "After just a few months, it slowed down so much, and then it went downhill from there." In their last year together, they'd made love only once.

Ten years into the relationship, Shelley began to wonder if she was missing her chance for a fulfilling sexual life. She wanted to feel more alive, and to feel more affection from her partner. But Jan liked things as they were, and when Shelley complained about how rarely they had sex, she often responded along the lines of, "We're pretty normal for lesbians."

Shelley wanted to be understanding and supportive, but her desire for intimacy got the better of her, and she found herself contriving all sorts of situations and ways to persuade or coerce Jan into sex.

Eventually, Jan began to feel angry about being pressured so much and lashed out with, "How can I feel sexual toward you? You're always trying to control me!"

Control: that was what it boiled down to, for both of them. Each of them felt the other was too controlling. From Jan's perspective, Shelley was being self-centered and insensitive, trying to manipulate her into having sex. Shelley, of course, saw it differently. She pointed out that Jan was the one who was getting what she wanted most of the time. When Jan didn't want sex, which was most of the time, sex wasn't happening. Like

>

Jan, Shelley also felt manipulated, because Jan would sometimes hint at things like, "Maybe this weekend we can take some time together." Then the weekend would arrive, and Jan would be in a bad mood and not at all open to sexual intimacy. This pattern of buildup and letdown was more than just a tease from Shelley's perspective. It hurt. Eventually, Shelley began to feel victimized by Jan's moods. It was made worse by inter-mittent reinforcement: However rarely, Jan would sometimes "give in" and have a sexual encounter with her. Each time that happened, Shelley thought, *It's a good thing I kept asking and asking.* It kept her hoping for more, and it reinforced her pressuring behavior.

Eventually Shelley thought of a new tactic. She proposed an experi-ment, saying she wouldn't initiate sex for the entire summer. "Since you feel so pressured," she said, "I'm going to stop asking you. If you want to make love, you ask me." Shelley kept to her word. She stayed available, but she didn't ask, suggest, or hint. She actually hoped the lack of pres-sure would help Jan be more interested in approaching her. Jan seemed pleased with this arrangement. She laughed and teased Shelley about it, often hinting that she would be initiating sexual contact soon. But she didn't, and their sexual relationship ground to a halt.

Before long, Shelley was having an affair. She still loved Jan and felt terribly guilty, but the intimacy and attention she needed was finally being fulfilled. Even though Shelley recognized, fairly quickly, that she didn't have enough in common with the new woman to form a new relation-ship, she did recognize how important sex was to her. She wasn't willing to live a nonsexual life anymore. For her part, Jan was too hurt and angry to work things out. They parted, amicably but sadly.

Both Shelley and Jan would have benefited from a frank discussion of how and why sex mattered to each of them. For Shelley, sexual inti-macy invited both physical and emotional connection. She enjoyed sexual contact a great deal and seemed very in touch with her physiological

>

sensations and urges. Sharing this pleasure with someone she loved fostered emotional intimacy and reinforced her commitment to her partner.

Jan did not have the same associations to sexual intimacy. Because it was rarely on Jan's radar screen, she didn't see sexual intimacy as something intrinsically fulfilling for herself. She enjoyed sexual experiences when they happened but didn't linger over pleasurable memories. She rarely masturbated or thought about sex at all. Jan didn't think of sex as a way to deliberately create feelings of emotional connection. To her, that was an almost accidental byproduct.

If Shelley and Jan could have talked about these differences in a nonjudgmental way, they could have decided, as a couple, how much sex would matter in their relationship. They would have needed to respect that their perspectives were equally valid. There is no "correct" amount of physiological drive, or emotional intensity, required for a successful relationship. At the same time, sex does add a specific type of intimacy that many women cherish and don't want to live without. Appreciating both of these perspectives would have helped Jan and Shelley make more conscious decisions along the way, instead of drifting into stagnant waters. For example, they could have decided that sex mattered just enough to commit to two dates a month and to be completely positive and supportive of each other in the sexual arena. They could have worked as a team, trying to nourish what they wanted to sustain.

WHEN IT COMES to desire discrepancy, I am always reminded that there are two sides to the story and two valid sets of feelings. Did one pull away because the other badgered her too much? Or did one badger because the other had pulled away? It's often impossible to know exactly how the dilemma started. In some ways, this kind of dilemma starts even before a couple first meets. Two women trying to sustain sexual intimacy confront a lot of antisexual forces. There are taboos about women being too sexual, taboos about having sex with other women, and demeaning cultural messages about women who are pleasure-centered. And then there are the demands of everyday life—work, family, friends, other interests. These are all important, but they can be antisexual forces too, because they take up so much time that there's little left for a partner. Those are the real enemies of sexual intimacy, and if both partners can let go of blaming each other and be more aware of the real culprits, they stand a much better chance of resolving the conflict.

Keep in mind that the goal in working with desire discrepancy isn't to coerce either partner into accepting something she doesn't want. It's to help both partners work out a sexual relationship that's good enough for both of them. The main challenge is to handle and accept differentness. That's not easy to do in any arena, but it's especially hard when it comes to sex.

There are so many negative labels for women: "frigid," "addicted," "inhibited," "compulsive," "withholding," "too loose," "too uptight." We are far too quick to apply these labels when something differs from what we want or expect. That's why the first step in working on desire discrepancy is to help couples stop judging and start validating each others feelings. No one's perfect, and no one has the perfect sex life, but there are couples whose sexual relationship is good enough to keep them both feeling satisfied with themselves and with each other. They approach their differences as a team whose goal is to sustain an intimate relationship.

So what if sex *isn't* your goal at all? Why should you have to work toward something you don't care about? Those are fair questions. If you're absolutely certain that you don't ever want to have sex again, you should let your partner know this, so she can decide what she needs to do. But the problem I usually encounter isn't that one person has definitely decided not to have sex again. It's that she thinks she might someday, but not now. This is what keeps both partners in sexual limbo, with the possibility of resolution just out of reach.

With all due respect to anyone who feels like she shouldn't have to have sex if she doesn't want to, I have to point out one thing. Sex is a reasonable expectation in a committed, primary relationship. Some people bristle at the word "expectation," but let's be real. We have lots of expectations in a relationship; for example, we expect to share emotional support, vacations, expenses, and household duties. It would be a problem if one of us announced, "I don't want to give you emotional support anymore, so don't expect it." Why should it be different when it comes to sex? Obviously it's less important to some people than others, but most couples start a new relationship with sexual activity. Unless you've been explicit that you don't plan to continue, it's reasonable for your partner to anticipate more sex with you.

On the other hand, even though sex is a reasonable expectation, it is not reasonable to expect someone to want to make love with you if you're harassing and criticizing her for not being sexually available. I've been amazed at some of the disrespectful ways women talk to the partners they're wanting to make love with. These women need to keep in mind that there is nothing wrong with their "low desire" partner—in fact, "low desire" is quite "normal." As mentioned in chapter 1, the Laumann studies found that at least one-third of women have "low desire."[1] Given that it's so common, many sex therapists and researchers no longer consider this a sign of psychological dysfunction or deficient mental health. Instead, it's considered normal. It isn't appropriate to label someone who has lower desire with a diagnosis or even to suggest that she has a psychological problem. She may have a relationship problem, because she and her partner are different in this regard, but there isn't anything intrinsically "wrong" with her.

What are the implications of this data? When we discuss this research in the couples' intimacy workshops, most women have one of two reactions. The "low desire" women look relieved, and say "I thought I was the only one!" The "high desire" women are also usually very surprised and relieved to learn that so many women express little interest in sex. This new information can be very helpful in the sense that their partner's low desire no longer seems like such a personal rejection. But it can also be demoralizing for them. I often see a look of shock and disappointment, and hear things like, "Does this mean this is as good as it gets?"

Not at all. It just means that you both need to stop labeling each other on the basis of how much you like sex. Feeling bad about yourself doesn't help you feel more sexual, and being critical of your partner doesn't make her want you more. On the contrary, negative judgment will dampen whatever flicker of sexual interest might exist. If you and your partner truly "get it" that plenty of normal, attractive, intelligent women simply don't think about sex that much, you can choose to be intentional about this. You can even decide to accommodate each other, without losing your sense of autonomy or self-respect.

Arica and Madison struggled with desire discrepancy for several years. Arica longed to linger in bed on weekend mornings, drinking coffee, talking, and making love, while Madison often seemed nervous and quick to mention other tasks that needed to be done. For a long time, Arica managed to persuade Madison to stay in bed with her at least every other weekend. She felt a little bad that it seemed to take such an effort to get Madison to stay. They had long talks about this issue, with Madison usually saying she just felt nervous; she enjoyed sex when it happened but had a hard time remembering that the next time there was an opportunity. For a long time, Arica attributed Madison's reluctance to her religious upbringing. Later, though, she began to wonder if Madison just wasn't attracted to her any more. She found herself watching Madison around other women, to see if she showed more interest there. A few times she asked Madison if that was the problem. Madison was offended by the question and told Arica that her insecurity was unbecoming. This discussion felt terrible to Arica, and she backed away from Madison sexually for several weeks.

Later Arica returned and began again to initiate sexual contact on weekends. Madison again responded, reluctantly, and they resumed their relationship, although with sex less frequently than before. And then a puppy arrived, and things changed again.

Madison loved the puppy. She began to jump out of bed early every morning—including weekends—to take the puppy for a walk. Sometimes she told Arica to stay in bed and wait for her to come back, but Arica felt insulted by this suggestion. Besides, the puppy walks got longer and longer. While Madison was out with the puppy, Arica mulled over some painful thoughts. *She cares more about the puppy than me. She doesn't act like she misses sex at all. She seems relieved to have an excuse to get away from me. She's been acting happier since she got the puppy.*

When Arica talked to Madison about these thoughts, the discussion did not go well. Madison got angry and told Arica that her morning walks

>

were the best part of her day. She also accused her of being needy and controlling. This hurt Arica deeply. She felt like she'd turned into a wimpy, pleading child, and that it was time to stop. She signed up for a tennis team that practiced every weekend, in the morning.

The first time Arica went off for tennis practice, she hoped that Madison would notice and say something. She did, but it was something that felt meaningless, like, "Have a good time." For Arica, Madison's lack of reaction was the final blow. She resolved that she had to accept that Madison just wasn't interested in a sexual relationship with her. She decided to stop making any overtures to Madison, ever, and went through a few weeks of quietly grieving the loss of her dreams for sexual intimacy. For a while, she tried to just focus on improving her tennis game and began going out for lunch after practice with several of the other players.

When one of the other players flirted with her, Arica felt very flattered. She felt her heart flutter a bit and smiled for the rest of the day. Later that week, Arica went to a party and was surprised to find the other woman there. They flirted some more, then went on the deck and kissed. Arica felt guilty and resolved to stay away from this woman. That worked, for three days. Then they met again and had sex.

After the sex, Arica had an empty feeling. She didn't really like this woman that much and knew she'd been responding to her own hunger for sexual attention. Part of her longed to tell Madison about it, but she knew that would be the end. So she pulled herself together, went home, and resumed her platonic relationship with Madison.

It was interesting to Arica to notice, a few weeks after her liaison with the other woman, that Madison no longer walked the puppy every morning. It occurred to Arica that she could try to start up some sexual contact again, except her heart wasn't in it. She felt like the flicker of interest had finally died, and she just wasn't interested enough to get it going again. She lived with Madison for another year, until she met someone else and moved on.

If you're "low desire," you can choose sexuality—not because you're deficient or inferior, but because you want the added rewards that sexual intimacy brings to a relationship. After all, many "low desire" women agree that sex is great once it gets going, and that when it's over, they're glad it happened. Just to illustrate the point that we can be motivated to do something we don't feel a "natural desire" for, I'd like to point out that I rarely want to do physical exercise—until I get started. Before then, I even have little arguments in my head, in which I'm rebelling against an imaginary authority figure who's telling me I have to go for a run. "No, I don't!" I shout. "You can't make me!" Then I laugh, because the imaginary authority figure is just the smarter part of me who knows how good I'll feel later if I exercise. Once I start running, I will love how I feel, and I'll remind myself of this the next time I don't want to exercise. If I waited for the "natural desire" to exercise, it would almost never happen—and I'd be much less happy. But thinking I'm abnormal for not having that "natural" urge to run would be silly and nonproductive.

A discrepancy in sexual desire challenges two women in the places where we are most conflicted. You had to learn the right to say "No!" to unwanted sex, but now I'm suggesting that sometimes you need to say "Yes!"—even if you don't feel like it. You need to trust your feelings and also listen to objective data: Most of the time, sex is good for relationships.

MANY OF THE women who have come to talk with me about their sex lives—or lack thereof—are actively considering leaving the relationship. Sometimes they are already involved with a new partner and realize they can't accept a sexless life. Other times they are trying to make a rational decision. They are usually struggling with two issues in particular: "How much have I already invested, emotionally and financially?" And "What are my alternatives, if I leave this relationship?"

The emotional investment is usually heavy. Women who have been together for several years often say they love the other as "my best friend," the person with whom they spend the most time and share the most activities. They know each other's histories and vulnerabilities. They've met each others families and often feel emotionally connected to them as well. Their mutual friends see them as a couple and would be heartbroken if they broke up. And they dread the idea of being alone. Is it worth going through the emotional turmoil in hopes of enjoying more sex?

Financial investments are also a factor to consider. Many women have bought homes together, have opened joint bank accounts, and share credit cards, vacation homes, timeshares, boats, cars, and other big-ticket items. Besides the ordeal of separating all those joint assets, they face the reality that living alone usually costs more than sharing expenses. Again, they wonder, *Is the pursuit of an elusive sex life worth a reduction in my standard of living?*

The concept of "elusive" relates directly to beliefs about lesbian sexuality. Women may think, *If everyone stops having sex after a few years, why bother changing partners? Just stay with the one you have, enjoy the emotional and financial benefits, and let sex go.* The underlying question here is, "What are my chances of finding someone who likes sex as much as I do?" I've known many women who stay suspended in this decision-making process for a long time, until they either resign themselves or meet someone new.

Of course, this is a moot point if the woman has already begun a new sexual relationship. In that case, she's probably enthralled and much further down the road toward a breakup, unless there are obvious problems with the new lover. She doesn't actually have an accurate picture of how sex will persist, because it's still new, but the power of immediate pleasure is probably going to override rational thinking at this point.

I'VE JUST DESCRIBED a sad process. Two women who started out diving into hot sexual currents together ended up drifting too far apart, until one started to wonder, *Could there be more?* But a better question, I think, is "Can you have more with your partner? What would it take?"

What it takes is teamwork and a game plan. Sexual teamwork gives women a unique opportunity to tackle a classic female problem: *How do I respect her wishes without abandoning my own? How do I give enough without giving too much? How do I hold onto you, and me, at the same time?* These questions are front and center in the sexual arena, and the rewards are wonderful if you focus on the game plan. Sexually active couples collaborate with each other to fulfill their unique sexual mission.

Perhaps you haven't thought of sex as a mission. By "mission," I mean that you and your partner share a common goal and agree on objectives that help you reach that goal. And the goal is to develop a sexual relationship that's satisfying to *both* partners.

You and your partner need to talk about your goals and what kind of rules will work for both of you. There's no need to evaluate each other's psychological fitness or sexual maturity—just talk about your sexual mission. How often would you like to have sex with each other? If you both agree on once-a-week, once-a-month, once-a-year, or never, that's great—if it's truly okay for both of you. If one of you wants sex every day, and the other every month, you have some talking to do. That's a big difference to bridge. Just don't kid yourself that sex will "just happen" because you love each other. There's too much research and experience to confirm that it won't.

It's also about being nonjudgmental, toward both yourself and your partner. Instead of judgment, how about compassion? You're both women, and you've both been subjected to plenty of negative messages about sexuality. If you've internalized a few of those, welcome to the human race! Who hasn't? Instead of reacting negatively toward each other's differences, try reacting with compassionate support, as a team, to overcome this challenge together. It's a serious one, and it deserves your best efforts.

Your Turn

① In your primary relationship, who seems to have the most sexual desire? Would both of you agree about this? Are you both open about this, or is it an "unspoken truth"?

② When did you notice that there was some difference between you and your partner in terms of desire levels? How long after you got together? Do you remember how you felt when you realized this? Were you worried? Disappointed? Sad? Angry? Indifferent? Relieved? Any other feelings? How did your partner feel about it? Do you remember talking with her about it, and how that went?

③ How would you guess that you and your partner feel about your desire levels at this point in your relationship? Is this something you can talk about? Does talking about this seem productive or helpful?

④ If there are significant differences in your desire levels, what kinds of things have you attempted to do to resolve these differences, so that both of you feel good enough about your sexual relationship? How have these efforts worked out? Pretty well, a little bit, or not at all?

⑤ Consider talking to your partner about creating a Sexual Mission Statement together. What does it mean to each of you? Why is it important? What frequency do you think would be enough? How much can you commit to this as a goal?

4

Body Image & the Tyranny of Weight

AT THE BEGINNING of each sexual intimacy workshop, I ask participants to complete several questionnaires. One of these asks women to rank the most negative influences on their sexual relationship. For over *half* of the workshop participants, "negative body image" heads the list of negative influences.

Specifically, these women say that they perceive themselves as being overweight, and that this interferes with their ability to enjoy sexual encounters. They say they are very self-conscious, and that they feel and express disdain—or even self-hatred—about their weight. Very often, their partners shake their heads in disbelief, saying, "But I like your body! If I didn't, I wouldn't want to make love with you." Partners may offer reassuring comments such as, "You look good to me," or "I enjoy your voluptuousness," or even, "I can't believe you think that about yourself." Sadly, those reassurances are usually to no avail. Most women also express some dissatisfaction with some other physical features, such as not liking their breasts or hips. But when women say they are afraid to take their clothes off in front of a lover, they're almost always talking about "feeling fat."

Throughout my career, I've encountered women of all shapes and sizes who have been indoctrinated with the idea that they don't deserve to have a sexual relationship if they're not thin. So many women feel unworthy, ashamed, and ostracized because of their perceived lack of physical perfection—despite the fact that, for better or worse, about two-thirds of all Americans weigh more than their doctors think they should.[1]

Sally was a striking young woman who attended one of my workshops with her slightly overweight partner, Lorraine. It was obvious that Sally had spent time in the gym. She was slim and fit, with sculpted biceps and muscular legs. But during the workshop, she seemed oblivious to the admiring glances coming her way. She looked sad and preoccupied . . . and Lorraine looked irritated.

As part of that workshop, each woman completed a questionnaire about her sexual concerns and dynamics in her relationship. Sally's and Lorraine's responses were enlightening. Lorraine had less interest in sex than Sally. And despite her toned body, Sally was afraid she was overweight, that her breasts were too small, and that her skin wasn't perfect. She thought if only she could "look better," Lorraine might be more interested in sex. Lorraine, on the other hand, was annoyed that Sally worried about her body so much and said it was hard for her to enjoy sex with someone who was so consumed with perfection. "I feel like she's more worried about how she looks than about how I feel," Lorraine said.

There's a saying that goes, "Sometimes the solution becomes the problem." This was what had happened with Sally. Her problem was Lorraine's lack of sexual interest, and her solution was to "perfect" her body, thinking this would make her more attractive. Thus Sally's focus was directed at herself and her physical appearance. Not only did Sally's solution to the problem fail, but it also exacerbated it, as Lorraine was turned off by what she saw as self-centeredness in Sally. It became a vicious cycle.

>

When Sally and Lorraine talked with each other about what each had written on her questionnaire, both were very surprised. Sally was shocked to realize that Lorraine perceived her as being obsessed and self-centered about her body. It hadn't occurred to Sally that worrying about how she looked made her less emotionally available to Lorraine because her energy was caught up in criticizing herself. In fact, she wasn't even really looking at Lorraine. Her inward focus didn't allow her to notice how her behavior was affecting her partner.

Although she felt chagrined at first, Sally rose to the occasion, saying, "A light bulb just went on!" She realized that it is more loving to pay attention to your partner than it is to focus on how you can look better to her. She could also see how that kind of loving attention was more likely to enrich their sexual connection than endless ruminations about her own body.

Lorraine also had a moment of insight as she and Sally talked about what each had written on the questionnaires. Because she had felt irritated by Sally's preoccupation with her body, Lorraine had stopped giving Sally any compliments. She had been afraid that saying something like, "You really look good!" would reinforce Sally's perfectionism. As they talked about this pattern, Lorraine also rose to the occasion. She admitted that withholding positive feedback was a passive-aggressive way to punish Sally for being so self-absorbed. She even realized that being more generous in her compliments would probably help Sally worry less and connect more.

Media images of physical perfection bombard us, and the pressure for women to be beautiful is intense and pervasive. Of all the criteria for female beauty, the most stringent one is to be thin. In addition to cultural pressures to be thinner, we are bombarded with information about the medical risks associated with excessive weight—heart disease, diabetes, and cancer are mentioned most often. Some researchers suggest that the risks of obesity exceed those associated with smoking, and some companies provide incentives to their employees to exercise and lose weight in order to reduce costs of health insurance. Unfortunately, this may just add to the stigma and discrimination against overweight people.

Women categorized as overweight experience prejudice at every level. They are less likely to be selected as friends, less likely to get hired or promoted, less likely to be accepted to college and graduate school, and less likely to achieve success in almost any endeavor.[2]

It's hard to overstate the societal stigma of being overweight in today's society. And it's important to take special note of that last phrase, "in today's society." In the past (and even today in some cultures), being plump and pale was a sign of prestige, affluence, power, and nobility—these people were the "sex symbols." The assumption was that these people had enough money and free time to enjoy the finer pleasures of life, such as good dining. People who were fit and tan were those who had to work hard, usually outdoors, perhaps in the fields. In today's socioeconomic structure, being fit and tan are not equated with hard labor. Instead, people who are fit and tan are equated with affluence, presumably because one needs plenty of free time and money for gyms, personal trainers, tanning beds, and long beach vacations.

Though it's not a completely safe haven, being overweight inside the queer community has far less of a stigma than it does outside of it. Perhaps because we are on the receiving end of intolerance, we are more supportive of individual differences and less likely to judge others based on superficial features. The strong feminist values that many of us share guide us to focus more on personality and behavior, less on physical attributes. We all know women, straight and gay, with partners who exemplify nonphysical qualities, such as warmth, intelligence, power, status, creativity, and kindness. Because we're less likely to relate to men sexually, we're less likely to restrict our eating just to satisfy stereotypically male criteria for thin "trophy wives." Those of us who did restrict ourselves in the past in order to meet those criteria may take extra pleasure in being more "indulgent" in the present. Perhaps these things explain why lesbian women are twice as likely to be obese as straight and bisexual women.[3]

Tara, a successful corporate attorney, admitted to me in a session that she hadn't been to a doctor in more than six years. When I asked why, she began to weep. "It's that horrible scale," she said. "They always weigh you."

Tara was only moderately overweight, but there was nothing moderate about her shame. She judged herself harshly for gaining weight and assumed that everyone else shared her disdain for her body. Tara's admission about avoiding the doctor opened the door for her to work on her shame about her weight, and it was the beginning of a therapeutic growth spurt. She talked about how she had withdrawn socially and avoided opportunities to meet other women because she was sure no one would be interested in "a big person like me."

As Tara listened to herself, she was amazed at all the different ways her body image—not her body—had affected her life. And she found the courage to schedule an appointment for a medical examination.

Tara's physician was caring and sensitive about issues of weight and shame. She listened carefully as Tara described her lifestyle, including her

>

eating and exercise patterns, and then suggested some minor changes that helped Tara develop healthier habits. For example, she suggested that Tara walk her dog a little farther and faster. But the goal of exercise, the doctor said, was not to lose weight, but to feel better. Weight loss may be a byproduct, she said, but that benefit is almost incidental to the more important goal of improving one's sense of well-being.

Tara was astounded. In retrospect, the doctor's point seemed simple and obvious to her, but her shame and self-disdain had been clouding her perspective, painting exercise as something she should do to lose weight. It hadn't occurred to her that she'd simply feel better, whether she lost weight or not.

With this different perspective, Tara began a new phase in her life. She did begin to walk more briskly, and she noticed within days that she felt better in her skin. She found herself being more outgoing, even striking up conversations with strangers on her walks. One of those strangers turned out to be a lesbian neighbor who'd had her eye on Tara. Though the attraction wasn't mutual, Tara realized that she was desirable and interesting. That boost gave her the courage to start attending some lesbian events, during which she eventually met a woman and fell in love. Her new sexual relationship with her partner was even more affirmation for Tara. She felt how much her lover enjoyed her body, and this helped her accept and appreciate herself more.

I'm no longer in touch with Tara, and I don't know if she ever lost any weight, but she certainly did lose the shame that was preventing her from claiming her share of social and sexual attention.

It's great that we're more accepting and less judgmental. We need that. However, we also we need to be realistic about the health risks associated with obesity, as well as the overwhelming prejudice faced by women who are overweight. Women who are obese face significantly higher risks for serious medical problems, such as diabetes, heart disease, and cancer, as well as knee and back problems associated with carrying extra weight. These risks add to the prejudice against overweight women; for example, potential employers may expect more healthcare costs or limited mobility. These prejudices are often not verbalized directly, but we can be sure that they are operating in the minds of people selecting applicants for jobs, or training programs, or even friendship networks.

Physical risks of obesity are evident, but it's the psychological pain that is most tormenting. In hundreds of conversations with women who struggle with their weight, I've heard one thing repeatedly: They want to hide because of the shame.

No matter the reason for our propensity for extra body fat, the more important factor is that many of us experience the double discrimination of being queer and overweight. Our sexuality is already devalued because we orient toward other women, *and* we're indoctrinated to believe that only thin people are sexy. These are strong, antisexual messages coming from our culture. It isn't surprising that we do to ourselves what our culture does to us—internalize the disdain for our bodies, feel bad about ourselves, and withdraw from others.

However, I want to make sure I'm very clear about this, as I think it's a common misconception. Body *type* does not affect your sex drive. Body *image*, however, most certainly does. There are women of all shapes and sizes with a high level of sexual desire, and there are women of all shapes and sizes with low desire.

During my intimacy workshops, a couple things almost inevitably happen: At some point, a thin woman will start talking about her lack of sexual desire. And at another point, someone will talk about wanting more sexual intimacy with her overweight partner. Some overweight women radiate positive sexual energy, and some thin women are rather asexual. I think that's something we all know, but this fact really stands out in the framework of the all-women sexual-intimacy workshops, and some people are surprised to realize that they have been conflating body type with body image.

Even if people don't realize on a conscious level that *actual* sex appeal (as opposed to our ideas about it) has little to do with physical features, they do realize it on a very personal and subconscious level. Studies done by social psychologists have confirmed that interpersonal responsiveness is more important than physical standards of beauty when it comes to attraction. One experiment illustrating this was conducted with male college students. Each young man was invited to attend a meeting. When he arrived, he was told to wait in the lobby until he was called. While he was waiting, a young woman would come in and sit down with him. Unbeknownst to the student, the woman was actually part of the experiment, and there were actually two women playing this role: one with striking physical beauty, and the other average-looking. The beautiful one was instructed to interact minimally with the student, and the average-looking one was instructed to be appropriately friendly, to smile, to make eye contact, and to respond with interest to the young man's communication. After fifteen minutes, the young man was called in and asked a series of innocuous questions. Then the interviewer asked him if he had noticed the young woman sitting next to him, and how much would he like to have a date with her. To a significant degree, the young men said they would prefer a date with the average-looking, socially responsive young woman.[4]

I see this sort of thing all the time in my workshops. In the beginning, when women first come in, they check each other out quite thoroughly. There are a lot of covert glances, especially toward the women who fit the most typical standards of physical beauty. But after we get started, the interpersonal behaviors start to stand out. Women who seem attentive, who listen and respond to others, become very attractive. Others begin to look and smile at them more, respond positively to what they say, and even physically lean toward them more. Openness and warmth attract positive attention much more than physical features.

You may remember some instances like this yourself. Perhaps you were attending a class, or a community event, and first noticed people who were very physically attractive. As time went on, you began to feel more drawn to people who seemed intelligent, attentive, courteous, or kind. Making eye contact, smiling, friendliness, attentiveness—these are the things that draw people in.

Unfortunately, those attractive behaviors do not come naturally to people with a poor body image. Out of an instinct for self-protection, people with low self-esteem are more likely to have an internal focus, failing to interact much with their surrounding people and environment and failing to notice things that would normally give people a boost in their self-esteem. They are also more likely to fall prey to another defense mechanism: projection.

When she started therapy in her early forties, Vivian weighed a hundred pounds more than she wanted to. She'd been overweight for most of her life, with little moral support. She felt ashamed of her body, ashamed to be nude, and ashamed to have sex with her partner, Jill. She loved Jill and felt guilty for depriving her of pleasure, but that wasn't enough to override her shame and anxiety. Early in their relationship, Vivian was surprised that Jill wanted her sexually. She initially felt thrilled and grateful, and she began to enjoy sex for the first time in her life. But as the novelty faded, her old feelings of self-disdain came back to the surface, and Vivian gradually lost interest.

For her part, Jill was not judgmental about body weight. She was not bound to cultural perceptions of thinness. She worried about the medical risks associated with obesity, but she understood how painful the topic was for Vivian and refrained from being critical. What bothered Jill was not Vivian's weight so much as her reluctance to be sexual because she felt bad about how she looked. At some point, it began to hurt Jill's feelings that Vivian couldn't get past this enough to meet her halfway in the bedroom. Jill fluctuated between feeling resentful that Vivian couldn't "get over herself" and feeling resigned to a low-sex relationship.

One day Vivian came to a session and started talking about her vacation with Jill in Provincetown. "I don't know what got into me!" she exclaimed. "I felt so *sexual!* I never feel like that. But for that whole week, I did, and I loved it. So did Jill! She was amazed!" Vivian talked about how great it was to be in a town so dominated by gay people. But she also talked about how great it was to be surrounded with other queer women of her build. "There were all different sizes," she said, "short and tall, large and small. I saw women who looked like me laughing and having a good time. And I noticed that a lot of them were pretty sexy, and they weren't trying to hide it, or their bodies, at all. And they were having so much fun!"

>

One night, Jill and Vivian went to a lesbian bar, and once again, Vivian saw plenty of larger women there, dancing vigorously on the packed dance floor. She was inspired. "I usually feel too self-conscious, but seeing them made me get up and dance with Jill too. I would never have done that if those other women hadn't been out there." When Jill started acting frisky, Vivian thought "Why not!" She felt more in the mood than she had in years, and she enjoyed their sex more than she had in years. She even initiated a couple times during their vacation, which totally shocked Jill.

Listening to Vivian, I noticed how she kept emphasizing, *There were so many women who looked like me.* That was what turned her toward sexual contact with Jill. It wasn't just the gay-affirmative environment or the sunny days on the ocean that helped her feel sensual and relaxed. What stood out for her was the presence of so many women who looked like her.

That Provincetown vacation was a small but meaningful turning point for Jill and Vivian. One week didn't completely transform Vivian's lifelong feelings of shame about her body, but it did give her a very concrete, pleasurable experience to remember. Vivian really held onto her realization that "women like me" can have fun and feel sexual. She became more intentional about looking around at lesbian gatherings and noticing the range of bodies and relationships. As for Jill, she was just happy that something clicked for Vivian. She suggested Provincetown again for their next summer vacation.

If you are prone to projection, you are prone to misinterpreting the behaviors of others in a way that reinforces your worst fears. Like a sad movie reflected on a white screen, you project your *own* negative judgments about yourself onto others. In other words, if you judge yourself harshly, you assume—mistakenly, and often unfairly—that others do too. If you think of yourself as unworthy and unsexy because of your weight, you assume everyone thinks the same. It's very easy to forget that this is your own imagination and very easy to have strong emotional and behavioral reactions to what you're imagining others are thinking of you. It gets you to make very convoluted conclusions about yourself and others. It's a distortion of reality and serves no good purpose.

So how does one snap out of this vicious cycle? The goal here is not to "stop feeling so negative and bad about yourself." That can feel like an impossible goal. The better, and much more achievable first step, is to do things that naturally turn your inward focus outward. Once that happens, you will automatically notice the obvious: Women of all sizes have pleasure, have partners, and have sex. You will see large women looking upbeat and small women looking depressed. It's one thing to be reassured with, "You're okay just the way you are," but it's another to actually *see* women of all kinds enjoying themselves in a physical, sensual way—being playful, walking in the sun, holding hands, and dancing. Really *looking* at your surroundings is wonderful, because it gets you out your fear-based imagination and back into the real world around you.

For most people, turning focus from inward to outward isn't a matter of flipping a switch. It usually takes intentional, concerted effort for a period of time. But there are some short cuts. There was a great saying that became popular during the 1960s cultural revolution: "Get out of your mind and into your senses." For people who feel particularly shy or fearful of being judged by people, this is a great start. When out walking, notice all the physical sensations you can. Notice the cool air or warm sun on your skin. Take a walk on the beach barefoot, feel the breeze in your hair, the sand between your toes. Some women find gardening a great way to come alive in their bodies.

Cycling, walking, even just taking some extra time to luxuriate in a long stretching session after a nap—all of these are ways connect with your body. Any form of exercise, from a slow walk to a game of squash, is excellent—not to lose weight, but simply because it's a guaranteed way to feel good. Yoga can focus your attention on your body sensations and helps you appreciate how your feet and legs carry you, how your arms lift for you. It helps you appreciate how your body feels, not how it looks. In fact, many women consider yoga a form of sexual foreplay and intentionally plan to practice or take a class before a planned romantic encounter. The experience of focusing loving attention on how your body moves and stretches and bends can open your mind to more sensual awareness. Once that's been accomplished, shifting attention toward sexual sensations comes naturally.

Paying loving attention to your own body may seem selfish, or self-centered, or even slightly weird. But remember the wonderful, intimate loop of sexuality. *My experience of sensual pleasure is exciting to my partner, and hers is to me. Awakening my senses makes me more responsive to her touch. Being in touch with my body helps me touch hers lovingly.* This is why self-focus isn't selfish. It's a generous gift for both of you.

Your Turn

① Thinking about an enjoyable physical activity can help you be more aware of how you can increase sensuality in your life. Take a few minutes to think about the last time you enjoyed a physical activity. It doesn't have to be exercise or an organized sport, just a time you remember think-ing, "This feels good!" Once you've recalled this time, ask yourself these questions. "Is this something I do often or rarely?" "Do I do it alone or with someone else?" "Would I enjoy doing it again?" Answering these questions can guide you toward simple ways to tap into sensual aware-ness every day.

② Make a list of activities that you know make you feel good physically, that focus your attention on feeling strong or on pleasurable physical sensations. Try to make the list as long as possible. Then check how often you're doing these things. Are there ways you could increase their frequency?

③ See if you can identify at least one thing you do every day that gives you a pleasurable physical sensation. Think of that as one thing that can make you more sensual!

④ If you have been hurt in the past by someone who was not interested in you for some physical reason, keep in mind that everyone has a right to set her own standards for attractiveness, and everyone has differ-ent standards. You can't know her reasons for placing a high value on looks—maybe she was criticized as a child or feels insecure about her intelligence. What you can know is that if you keep looking around and being responsive to women you like, you'll soon meet more people who reinforce the things you love about yourself and who will be happy to have an engaging, responsive partner.

⑤ Ask yourself how attentive and responsive you are to others. You'll feel great when you notice the power you have to give positive energy to others.

⑥ If your partner's body image is interfering with her ability to enjoy sex with you, ask her how you can help with this. Listen attentively. Don't judge or attempt to rescue her; just try hard to really understand what it feels like to be her. Then you can tell her what you love about her body. Don't be critical, and don't give false reassurance. Most of us are acutely aware of insincere compliments. Be sincere in what you say, and be loving about it. You may even ask her to read this chapter and talk with you about it.

⑦ The following is a meditative exercise. Sit comfortably or lie down, close your eyes, and focus on your breathing for a few minutes. When you feel yourself to be in a more relaxed state, start by imagining that you are holding something you don't like about yourself in your hands. Look at what it is in a very gentle light of awareness. Instead of avoiding or turning away, keep your attention there in a nonjudgmental, accepting way. Your mind will probably wander into internal chatter from time to time, but the point is simply to notice when that happens and then refocus attention on breathing until you're ready to go back to the imagery. This exercise is both difficult and liberating. It's difficult because no one enjoys thinking about personal flaws and imperfections. But it's liberating because so much energy gets tied up trying to avoid exposing those flaws. When you stop judging yourself on unattainable criteria of physical perfection, that energy becomes available for more productive endeavors. This is what can happen when you look gently at the way you are.

5

Sexual Abuse & Trauma

IN EVERY ONE of my lesbian intimacy workshops, there has been at least one couple whose intimacy has been impacted by previous sexual trauma. Sadly, it's so prevalent that it's very likely you too have had friends or lovers who have suffered because of this, or that you yourself have. An appalling number of women and girls have experienced sexual offenses, including coercive and inappropriate sexual contact and acquaintance rape. With stranger rape, there is a special horror. In addition to the painful physical assault, the possibility of being killed is very real. In such cases, the victim almost certainly goes through post-traumatic stress disorder, experiencing nightmares, extreme anxiety, panic attacks, depression, withdrawal, and even hallucinations. These painful symptoms can linger for years, inhibiting sexual intimacy with a trustworthy partner. Recovering a positive sense of sexuality can be difficult, but it is definitely worth the effort.

Psychologist and author Judith Herman identifies two primary issues present after the trauma of sexual assault: feelings of isolation and feelings of helplessness.[1] Feelings of isolation are inherently a consequence of most sexual assaults, especially if the victim was alone with the perpetrator, because she doesn't have another person who can share her experience and say, "Yes, that was terrible for me too." There's also no one to validate her account and say, "Yes, that is what happened." Lacking that support, she feels terribly disconnected and vulnerable. She needs to talk about her trauma, repeatedly and in detail, with someone who believes her and helps her express the feelings she endured by herself. That's the way she can begin to heal from that terrible isolation—by feeling understood and connected to someone who cares for her. Sometimes, this can be a trusted partner who can offer a powerful sexually healing connection. At other times, friends or therapists can listen empathically without having their own feelings and needs complicate the issues. Some women feel the most connection when they talk in group therapy with others who have had similar experiences. Different kinds of healing relationships can help overcome the terrible isolation of trauma.

The other common emotion after trauma is helplessness. Women are often easily physically overpowered by their rapist and may be literally unable to prevent the attack. There is literally nothing she could have done—but that is very hard for the victim to accept, especially if she is an independent, take-charge person who never says "I can't." It can be a terribly cruel shock for her to realize how helpless she was, and it can leave her shaken to the core. Those feelings of helplessness can leak into other aspects of her life, making her feel helpless to recover from the trauma, to regain her life, and to reclaim her sexuality.

In such cases, it can help if the traumatized woman makes an effort to recognize ways in which she was not helpless, both during and after the assault. For example, she may have made choices about what to say and how to act that helped prevent further injury. Recognition of such choices can be empowering: They show an ability to think rationally and plan, even in the midst of a horrific ordeal. She can then come to healing conclusions: She couldn't prevent the attack, but she could, and did, take the best steps possible under those terrible circumstances. Even under dangerous pressure, she was able to think and act on her own behalf. Giving herself credit for this can strengthen her resolve to continue taking positive, empowering steps to recover from her trauma.

Women who have been assaulted as adults have some advantages when it comes to healing. Most will have already had the chance to develop a solid sense of self and possibly a loving relationship with an intimate partner. Those internal and external resources help them cope by giving them something strong and positive to return to.

One of the most moving encounters in my life was with a couple I met when I was on my internship in a Veterans Administration hospital.

Alina was a military chaplain and had been with her partner, Nadine, for eight years. They were stationed in a lovely seaside city, where Nadine taught high school and did a lot of volunteer work for their church. During most of those years, they lived off base in a gay-friendly neighborhood and were able to enjoy a fairly open lifestyle. They enjoyed their home and friends and felt very settled.

Then Alina got transferred. They had to uproot themselves, sell their home, move to a less desirable location, and start all over again with no social network, no friendly neighbors, and no job for Nadine. Alina felt guilty because she had caused so much upheaval. Nadine understood that

>

this was part of military life, but she couldn't help feeling resentful that her entire world had been turned upside down. Instead of working as a team, as they always had in the past, they were starting to direct their frustration at each other. This led them to seek professional help, and this is when I first met them.

I found them to be a delightful couple: considerate of each other and frank without being negative. They showed a lot of empathy for each other and didn't seem to get entrenched in rigid positions. I was impressed with their willingness to face painful issues directly. I was also impressed that Alina and Nadine had maintained an active sex life for their eight years together. Both said their intimate connection was a high priority for them, and that it helped to hold them together through other challenges. There was a strong undercurrent of trust and affection between them, even as they were struggling with all the losses and changes entailed in their recent move.

Three months after we started having sessions, they were feeling better. They had found another gay-friendly church, and Nadine had started doing some church volunteer work again. We stopped regular sessions with the understanding that they could come back any time.

About six months later, I had a tearful call from Alina. She told me that Nadine had been raped the week before. Nadine had been volunteering at the church, preparing snacks for a visit to a nursing home, when a man wandered in off the street. He grabbed her purse and started to leave. Reflexively, Nadine burst out, "Don't take that!" He stopped and came back to assault her sexually. After he left, Nadine called the police, who took her to the hospital and connected her with the rape crisis center. Alina had been by her side every step of the way. Nadine was better, but she was still struggling. She needed to talk.

The next sessions with Nadine were very painful. She had been having flashbacks and nightmares. She felt high-strung, startled easily, and found

>

herself making efforts to avoid any reminders of that terrible day. But in our sessions, she found, like most victims of assault, that she needed to tell the story of what had happened, including her terror and anger and grief about her ordeal. She also needed to work through her irrational self-blame. She kept saying, "I should have just let him take my purse . . . none of this would have happened." Nadine also blamed herself for being at the church alone. It was the middle of the day, and she had assumed other people would be around. She didn't realize she was completely alone until she called for help and nobody answered. Like so many women who have been sexually assaulted, Nadine felt ashamed, as if she must have done something wrong since this terrible thing had happened to her. She needed a lot of support to get over that irrational line of thinking. She began to get better as she redirected her fury toward her attacker. She also connected strongly with her determination not to let this assault destroy her loving, sexual relationship with her partner.

A few weeks later, Nadine said she and Alina were going away to the mountains for the weekend. She knew they needed to be sexual again, but she was afraid of how she'd react to being touched sexually after enduring such a trauma. She was also afraid of how Alina would feel. Would she seem repulsed? Pitying? Obligated? Nadine was scared, but she applied the same determination that she had shown about other issues: *This is important, so I'm going to show up.*

I felt afraid for Nadine and Alina. I didn't know if they could overcome this together, or if it would permanently damage their sexual relationship. I affirmed her desire to face this challenge and encouraged her to take her time and keep talking with Alina about what she was feeling. When Nadine came in for her first session after the weekend away, I was deeply touched.

Nadine said the weekend was wonderful. They took their time and blocked out all communication with the outside world. They cried—a

>

lot—as they talked about what had happened and how it had affected both of them. When they made love, Nadine felt overwhelmed by Alina's tenderness, relieved that both of them could feel sexually excited, and incredibly grateful to be together. They were very, very glad for the weekend.

At one point, Nadine looked at me through tears, and said, "I'll never forget being raped. But I'll never forget Saturday night, either."

Nadine's statement reflected two people at their absolute best. It would have been easy for both of them to just focus on keeping each other feeling as safe as possible and to avoid sex altogether. They could have concentrated only on emotional support but missed the empowering experience of actively initiating sexual contact. Alina could have taken a protective, parental role with Nadine but avoided sexual intimacy with her as a peer. Nadine could have pushed Alina away and asked for more time. Any of these reactions would have been understandable, but could have also prolonged the trauma. Instead they chose to face their fears directly, together, and they were rewarded with a life-changing moment of intimacy.

Soon after this, Alina requested and received another transfer. They were eager to leave a city that had brought so much trauma and glad that the new assignment was somewhere they both liked. I helped them identify counseling resources in their new location, in case either of them felt a need for more support. When they came in to say goodbye, I told them how much they had meant to me. They inspired me with their resilience and added fuel to my faith that we can overcome almost anything with courage and support. I'm forever grateful to them.

For women who were traumatized as children or adolescents, the road to recovery is usually more difficult. Young girls do not yet have the aforementioned coping mechanisms, and because their brains and their identities are still developing, the long-term impact on their development and personality can be rather deeply etched. The cognitive skills that are involved in good judgment keep developing until the early twenties.[2] Trauma occurring before then may inhibit normal development of good judgment. As a result, it may be hard for these women to recognize the danger in getting involved with self-centered, exploitative partners. Part of developing positive adult sexuality is learning to recognize which people are good for you and which ones you should stay away from. Ultimately, you're supposed to rely on your own judgment about who is trustworthy— but if you never got a chance to develop good judgment in the first place, you simply won't be able to do this.

Also, the childhood victim's sense of shame makes them vulnerable to partners who continue patterns of violating boundaries. When children and teens are sexually abused, there is always a level of physical or psychological coercion going on—and yet, many victims feel ashamed that they didn't resist more. Many children and teenagers overestimate their power to control events— children blame themselves when their parents divorce, while teenagers think they are immortal. This can grow into a belief that they are responsible for other people's bad behavior, and that if they try hard enough, they can get people to treat them better. That's a losing battle.

However, before I get too far into the impact of childhood sexual abuse and trauma, I want to first address some common myths associated with it. These were partially addressed in chapter 1 as well.

Lesbian women who have experienced childhood sexual abuse or trauma often wonder if it was the "cause" of their homosexuality—the thing that turned them away from men and toward women, perhaps for a what might be perceived as a safer sexual relationship. There's simply no evidence that this is true. Most women who were sexually abused as children grow up to be heterosexual, and most women who are lesbian were not sexually abused. There's no causal connection between sexual abuse and sexual orientation. There are *other* issues that seem significantly related to childhood sexual abuse, and I will get to them soon. But sexual orientation is not one of them.

When Ashley was thirteen, her mother was killed in a car accident. It was the first in a series of tragedies. She went to live with her father, stepmother, and her seventeen-year-old brother, whom she hadn't seen in eight years. It was a difficult adjustment. She was grieving the death of her mother, and it was obvious that her father and stepmother resented her presence. At one point, Ashley had to eat meals in her room because her father told her to stay away from his wife. She was a thirteen-year-old girl in an unfriendly home, with absolutely no one to confide in.

When her brother approached her sexually, Ashley was terribly conflicted. On the one hand, she knew this was incestuous and wrong. But she also felt desperately lonely and almost untouchable. Because she hadn't lived with her brother since she was five, she could pretend that he was just a teenage boy who was interested in her. The little bit of affection she felt from him made it okay for her, for awhile. She participated, and felt some physical pleasure, but she also felt guilty, ashamed, and afraid of what her brother would do if she told him to stop. For the three years that this continued, Ashley was alone with her shameful secret. She avoided teachers and peers at school and had a painful life at home.

>

At sixteen, Ashley confided in her high school counselor. The counselor contacted the local family services agency, which removed Ashley from the home. Her father and stepmother were furious with her and accused her of making up a story just to hurt them. Ashley went to live with a foster family.

This is when her luck began to improve. Her foster mother was a loving person, and Ashley developed a healthy attachment to her. With her encouragement, Ashley graduated from high school and started college. She also started attending a support group for sexual abuse survivors, which helped her feel less isolated and ashamed of her experiences. Ashley floundered some in college, dropping out and changing majors a few times, but she eventually graduated with a very marketable degree. She eased into her career and gradually built a stable, independent life for herself.

During her college years, Ashley tried relationships with both men and women, and she eventually acknowledged her primary lesbian orientation. She went through a stage of wondering if she was choosing women as a reaction to her bad experiences with her brother. Then she thought about all the women in her college support group who had also experienced sexual trauma and who were heterosexual. It clarified to her that sexual trauma didn't "cause" her sexual orientation. This knowledge removed a layer of stigma and helped Ashley move forward in her desire to find an intimate partner.

What emerged as a problem for Ashley was that she kept getting involved with partners who were self-centered and exploitative. Interestingly, the sexual part of the relationship was usually good, but the rest was not. Her first major relationship was with an alcoholic woman who used her to maintain financial stability. The second woman ran up major debts on Ashley's credit cards. The third woman was abusive, at first verbally and then physically.

>

In her fourth and final dysfunctional relationship, Ashley got involved with Mary, who had a teenage son. When Mary took a six-month job overseas, Ashley agreed to take care of her son. She rented out her own home and moved into Mary's house. Three years later, she was still there—struggling to pay her bills, on the verge of foreclosure, and cut off from her friends. Meanwhile, Mary had become increasingly critical and angry, and the teenage son was threatening violence. Ashley finally saw the light and left. She moved back into her own home and started going to therapy.

During her therapy sessions, Ashley explored the ways that some underlying shame was driving her into such unhealthy relationships. As a teenager, Ashley had felt very conflicted about her relationship with her brother: She felt guilty and ashamed but also enjoyed some physical pleasure. As an adult, Ashley reenacted her compromise between those different sets of feelings. She would let herself enjoy sexual pleasure with women who reinforced her guilt and shame by treating her so badly. She would also not notice how exploitative these women were until she was already entangled with them. Then she would be afraid to leave them because she assumed she'd have a hard time finding someone else to be with. It had taken the frightening experience of having Mary's son threaten violence for Ashley to comprehend that she desperately needed to make better relationship choices.

Being alone again was excruciating but better than living with Mary and her son. She found a second job and devoted one year to digging herself out of debt. Her single-minded focus paid off. After a year, Ashley was out of debt. She got a better job and began dating again. She noticed that she still had strong attractions to very self-centered women—but at least she noticed and was able to let go of these more quickly than in the past. She also learned not to jump to conclusions just because the sex felt good. Ashley came to realize that she could respond sexually to someone

>

who was not good for her, and that she needed to look for other criteria, such as empathy and trustworthiness.

After a couple years of dating different women, Ashley met someone she really liked and who was more like she was. Meredith was a very hardworking and responsible person who had achieved an admirable level of professional and financial success. She didn't need to exploit Ashley, because she could take care of herself. One limitation Meredith had was a lot of sexual inhibition. She had never been with someone who talked about sex comfortably. The years of work Ashley had done, recovering from her sexual trauma, helped her learn how to talk about sexual issues in a positive and nonjudgmental way. This was a gift for Meredith, and a gift for Ashley as well. She felt appreciated sexually, with no exploitation or coercion.

Five years after she began living with Meredith, Ashley was happy— and still surprised—about the emotional and sexual intimacy in her life. She told me she felt like a late bloomer, but laughed, saying "Better late than never!" Mostly, she felt grateful to have finally chosen a partner who treated her well.

Another myth is that childhood sexual abuse and trauma lead to low desire in adulthood. In fact, that's also not true. From my review of research on this topic, I've noticed there's very little, if any, evidence that abused women differ from the many nonabused women who report low sexual desire as adults. Sex researchers Julia Heiman and Cindy Meston addressed this question in their review of research on this topic.[3] (While the research was conducted with heterosexual women, there is no reason to assume results would be different among women who are lesbian.) The primary finding in all of the studies reviewed by Heiman and Meston is that women who were sexually abused as children are more likely to participate in risky sexual behaviors: sex with multiple partners, without adequate protection from sexually transmitted infections, or coupled with the abuse of drugs or alcohol. All of these behaviors are associated with a lack of self-protection.

This conclusion might at first seem counterintuitive. Why wouldn't women who have experienced abuse be even more careful, even more self-protective, than others? Several reasons may converge.

First, there's a great sense of shame involved in sexual abuse. These women often feel as if they're "damaged goods," and therefore less worthy of respectful treatment. Often, girls who are abused are told at the time that they deserve it, or that they provoked it, or even that they want it. Internalizing these untrue statements contributes to a negative sexual self-concept. When taking this shame into account, it's actually no wonder that in adult life many of these women tolerate disrespectful behaviors.

Another reason for risky sexual actions may be that these women feel as if it's futile to set limits or boundaries, since boundaries obviously weren't respected in the past. Children and teenagers don't get to say "no" to sexual perpetrators. One of the primary goals for people who have experienced any kind of sexual abuse is to learn how to set appropriate, flexible boundaries around sex. Unfortunately, often the reaction to abuse is to fluctuate between weak and rigid boundaries, neither of which support fulfilling and empowering sexual experiences.

Some children and adolescents who have been abused develop an inappropriate repertoire of sexual behaviors. They may learn to use sex to manipulate others. (This is fairly close to cultural standards of "femininity" anyway, as we see constant images of sexy women attracting wealthy men—in essence, trading sex for money.) We shouldn't be surprised that some young women who were rewarded early in life for being sexual then use sex as a tool to get needs met in adult life. Nor is it surprising that many of these women express hostility and cynicism toward their sexual partners, even while also being sexually aroused. As one client said to me, "My body would respond even though I knew what he was doing was wrong. That made me feel guilty, and mad at him for doing it. I knew he was using me but also knew I could get something out of him afterward if I promised not to tell. I still get mad sometimes today when I have sex, even though it doesn't make any sense." Given her history, it does make sense.

Rebecca and Michelle had lived together for eight years. They were both in their midthirties, and they had been sexually abstinent for the past five years. According to Rebecca, the first two years of their relationship had been fantastic, "a festival in the bedroom." Then sex dropped off the screen. "At first," said Rebecca, "I was really upset about it, because I wanted it much more than she did. We talked about it a lot, but then every time it seemed to turn into a fight, so I just stopped bringing it up. I still think about it sometimes, but it's not worth the risk to talk about. Talking hasn't gotten us anywhere."

Rebecca and Michelle were great friends and partners in every other way. Rebecca wished there were a way to feel sexually intimate with Michelle, but she doubted that could happen again. She seemed

>

to feel resigned and a little depressed about this, and said she couldn't help wondering if she just wasn't attractive enough for Michelle. Rebecca said she'd always struggled with low self-esteem, especially related to her looks. In Rebecca's previous relationships, she'd felt very self-conscious and rarely talked about sexual issues with a partner. She was impressed with how self-confident and attractive Melissa was, and she was thrilled when they became lovers. It helped Rebecca feel good about herself as a sexual partner, and she began to feel more confident in this arena. But when Michelle stopped being interested in sex, Rebecca's old feelings of being unattractive and unworthy of sexual attention came surging back, full force.

Michelle agreed that the first two years had been great. After that, however, she felt as though some unresolved issues from her past began to interfere. When she was a teenager, her father—a minister in a conservative Protestant church—began to touch her inappropriately and to make comments about her body. She began to avoid ever being alone with him, staying out late with friends and partying as much as possible. She thought about talking to her mother but was afraid of her reaction. She thought that her mother would blame her for being provocative or would be emotionally devastated, so she began to avoid her too. Gradually, Michelle developed a view of sex as something that was fun but dirty, secretive, and often associated with drugs and alcohol. She also learned to think of sex as a commodity that she could use to manipulate others as she had felt manipulated by her father.

"I don't know how to do long-term sex," Michelle said. "I know about sex when you're being wild, and partying, and feeling like you're using people or they're using you . . . but that feels like a different world, a long time ago." She said she loved Rebecca and thought of her as her best friend but just wasn't interested in sex anymore. She felt guilty, because she knew Rebecca was hurt by this, but she also felt unable to change.

Michelle had grown up with blatant confusion around boundaries. Her father espoused the rigid boundaries of strict, morally upright, conservative "family values," but he crossed sexual boundaries with his own teenage daughter. In response, Michelle set a new boundary with her father by staying away from home and in the company of other teenagers. Her adolescent sexual experiences involved weak boundaries with multiple partners and plenty of substance abuse. Then, as an adult, she developed a rigid sexual boundary with Rebecca—no sex at all, for five years.

What was completely missing in Michelle's sexual history was any opportunity to work out the kind of flexible boundaries that are needed in a long-term relationship. No one feels like having sex every time their partner wants to, but most of us are willing to make it happen at least some of the time. Being empowered isn't only about being able to reject coercive or manipulative sex. It's also about being able to choose sexual intimacy because you love your partner and know this is important to her. A gate that's always locked shut isn't more powerful than one that's always open. Both are a barrier to developing a sense of sexual empowerment in a loving, long-term relationship.

It also seemed that neither Rebecca nor Michelle was prepared for the inevitable decrease in sexual energy after their early romantic period faded. Each of them interpreted this in a way that contributed to more negative feelings. Both reverted to their respective preexisting conditions: Rebecca reverted to feeling unattractive, and Michelle reverted to feeling damaged by her father and her adolescent sexual experiences. Her statement "I don't know how to do long-term sex" suggests a sense of permanent deficiency. Neither of them had enough accurate information about female sexual desire to know that this was simply a natural progression that happens to almost everyone. Their negative interpretations left them both feeling helpless about their relationship and self-critical.

>

Michelle had started going to therapy to see if she could work through this barrier. She said that therapy had helped her understand how her father's inappropriate behavior had affected her and why she had such complicated feelings about sex. She had hoped that working through these issues would help her resolve the sexual impasse with Rebecca, but in the end, that didn't happen. Eventually, Michelle stopped therapy. She said she wanted to continue living with Rebecca because they shared so much, but she wondered how long they could last in this state of "celibate limbo." They stayed together for two more years, until Rebecca fell in love with another woman and moved out of the home. She and Michelle continue to be good friends.

Women who have experienced sexual trauma deserve to enjoy sexual intimacy with stable, loving partners. They need support, and courage, to face their fears and actively seek a corrective emotional and sexual experience. This is how they will overcome the terrible isolation of trauma and feel empowered to pursue and enjoy healthy sexuality. Through direct experience with a trusted partner, or through imagery or guided meditation, they can gradually work through the steps of allowing physical closeness and touch while maintaining a sense of control over the experience. They need to walk toward their fears—not away. Avoiding fears doesn't resolve them. They just get bigger, more entrenched, and more limiting.

This is frustrating not only for the women who experienced the trauma but also for the women who love them. It can feel difficult for these partners to know whether they're being appropriately supportive or whether they're letting the trauma ruin their chance at a fulfilling sex life. They are often torn between their own sexual desire and need for intimacy and a fear that any pressure to get these needs met might be damaging to their loved one. After all, most women are acutely sensitive to the trauma of sexual assault—we all know that it could happen to any of us, and even if we haven't experienced it personally, what we can imagine is horrific enough.

Sometimes a parent–child dynamic develops: The person who experienced abuse feels damaged and sexually inferior, and her partner is very protective but feels helpless to actually change anything. These roles are very understandable but also very antisexual. Neither a parent nor a child is an appropriate, desirable sexual object.

Our sensitivity, tenderness, and innate empathy with each other can be very healing, but it can also be counterproductive. If, out of love, a partner avoids or no longer initiates sexual intimacy with a partner who has been traumatized, no one wins. We need to feel empowered to seek sexual intimacy because it's something we enjoy, choose, and value. Avoidance is easier, but it keeps the trauma frozen in place.

The challenge is how to share painful experiences and express loving support without slipping into unhealthy roles that make you avoid adult sexuality. It's a difficult line to walk. So what is a loving, supportive partner to do? Well, she can start by getting more support for herself, similar to what is offered in Al-Anon meetings or some kinds of group therapy, where people are encouraged to focus on their *own* needs and feelings and to stop waiting for their partners to change. With this kind of support, these partners can make some decisions for themselves instead of hoping for a change in someone else. Sometimes women who have gone through this kind of trauma have given it a lot of thought and are pretty much sure they never want to be sexually intimate with anyone again. That's their right. In this position, their partners do have several choices: live with an asexual relationship, request a change in "the rules" in order to explore sexuality outside the relationship, or dissolve the relationship. The one choice they do *not* have is to change how their partner feels about sex.

Sometimes, these partners can convince their traumatized loved one to go to individual therapy, hoping that exploring their internal issues will release sexual energy. Unfortunately, this almost never happens. Instead, what usually happens is that the individual develops more understanding of why she is the way she is, but nothing changes in her sexual relationship. For this reason, sex therapist Jeanne Shaw says she works with sexual abuse issues in the context of couples' therapy. In individual therapy, she notes, ". . . the client bonds with the therapist—but she needs to bond with her partner, not me."[4] A therapist can give you undivided attention and a safe, supportive space one or two hours a week. But your partner lives with you, sleeps with you, and has needs of her own. Sexual intimacy requires teamwork, and teams do best when they practice together.

There's a very important, very positive point to remember. Most women who have been affected by sexual abuse *do* develop fulfilling sexual relationships at some point. It's easy to lose perspective because the stories and examples we hear are usually from women who don't feel able to move forward in an adult, sexual relationship. Many more have, and they value sexual intimacy even more because of their previous experiences. They understand how precious and affirming sexual contact can be because they've experienced the opposite and know the contrast. Abuse and trauma are *not* life sentences to dysfunction or celibacy. Resilience is a wonderful reality of the human condition. I've seen too many examples to ever doubt this.

Your Turn

① Have you had sexual experiences that made you feel isolated and helpless? Can you remember what helped you get through those? Have you given yourself credit for handling them the best way you could? Think about the different choices you could have made that might have caused even worse consequences. Notice that you're here right now, reading this chapter, instead of avoiding the whole topic!

② Do you think you're carrying isolated or helpless feelings into your current (or most recent) sexual relationship? How and when do you see yourself acting these out with your partner? Can you apply anything you learned from the answer above to help you? Are you making choices that could improve or worsen your current sexual situation? Do you remind yourself of the ways your current partner is *not* similar to people who have harmed you in the past? Can you talk to her about this?

③ What would you like your partner to understand about how your past sexual experiences have affected the way you are with her? Can you tell her this without diminishing yourself or putting her in the role of a parent? The purpose of this conversation is to be explicit about some unspoken feelings and concerns that you have with her—not to put yourself down or try to measure up to her approval. When you can talk as one adult to another about things that happened in the past, it will be easier for both of you to understand how you are both similar and different from each other. You'll feel more connected to each other while also respecting your differences.

④ If you've experienced sexual trauma, have you given yourself the time and space to resolve your feelings about it? Have you talked with someone you really trust to be caring and respectful, who will maintain appropriate boundaries with you while you discuss these sensitive issues? This could be a friend, partner, therapist, or spiritual adviser. Remember that secrecy often adds to shame. You have a right to privacy about these very personal issues, but it's important not to hide from everyone.

⑤ If you have a partner who has experienced sexual trauma, have you talked with her about how this affects you? You may be so concerned about her well-being that you ignore your own feelings, but that won't work in the long run. Your feelings are valid too. Remember that if you're overly worried about protecting her feelings, you're sliding into a parental role, which will destroy your sexual relationship. It's better to risk a little anxiety—and better yet to let a third party (like a helping professional) help both of you together, so you don't have to carry this burden alone.

6

Aging & Hormones

"OH, WELL, I'M just too old for that."

When I hear these words of resignation, I first cringe, then feel a surge of gratitude for my mother, who began a new career and lived a fulfilling and active life after she turned sixty. By the time she was eighty, she had lost some inhibitions and started telling me about how much she and my father had enjoyed sex in their old age. I had two reactions: "TMI!" (too much information) and "Go Mom!" One of her biggest gifts to me was her living example of how to age well.

I'm glad my mother didn't buy into cultural attitudes about aging and sex. Too many of us do. Our jokes about aches and pains, "senior moments," and sagging body parts reflect our anxiety about losing mental and physical fitness, attractiveness, and sexual vitality. Joking is a very human way to cope with things we can't escape. In this case, mortality. Aging happens, like it or not. And it can bring some wonderful gifts: appreciating the present moment, understanding what really matters, relishing those we love. These are gifts that can only enrich our capacity for sexual intimacy, at any age. Many lucky women know that these gifts can outweigh any negative factors associated with the physiological changes of aging.

When asked about the negative sexual effects of aging, most women think of hormones. Testosterone, estrogen, and progesterone are all involved in sexual arousal and orgasm—but I think these hormones have become the scapegoat for decreased desire in older women. True, there's a physiological component of desire that seems closely tied to hormone levels. Many women relate to this because they experience a surge of sexual urges a few days before the onset of menstruation, when estrogen and progesterone levels are changing. But what do they do with those urges? Fan the flames? Make plans to act on them? Set the stage for a sexual encounter? Physiological urges can generate sexual interest, but consummation requires intention and action, and it's more complex than hormones. It's important to keep the context in mind while understanding how changing hormone levels can impact sexual experiences.

Both estrogen and progesterone, at optimal levels, increase the flow of blood to the vulva and pelvic area. When these hormone levels decrease, so does the speed and volume of blood flow to those sexually sensitive areas. This causes physical responses to be slower and reduces chances for orgasm. Lower estrogen levels also contribute to thinning of vaginal and urethral tissue, which can cause recurrent urinary tract infections. Vaginal dryness is also related to lower estrogen levels. This can have a self-perpetuating effect: Being dry can make you feel uncomfortable and discouraged, which decreases your motivation to be sexual, which reinforces your image of yourself as an asexual person. Additionally, progesterone is a precursor of testosterone, which is the hormone most directly tied to sexual pleasure. Women who are prescribed testosterone for medical reasons, such as surgical removal of the ovaries (causing sudden onset menopause), can attest that it really helps them feel aroused and have orgasms.[1] Sexual activity increases testosterone levels, which makes sex more pleasurable, which increases motivation to have sex again, which increases testosterone levels. It's part of why we say "Use it or lose it."

Another age-related factor that women talk about is body image. Our bodies change in ways that may feel and look less attractive: We have less muscle, more fat, less tone, more wrinkles, less soft skin, more gray hair in unfamiliar places. We may appreciate maturity and seasoning, but cultural standards of sexiness and desirability are all about youth and beauty. Straight women are strongly confronted with this issue when they see men selecting much younger women as sexual partners. Lesbian women may be less harsh about it, but nevertheless, most of us would rather look younger, not older. As noted in chapter 4, how we feel about how we look has a big influence on the desire to engage sexually. Again, this sets up an unfortunate, self-perpetuating cycle: avoiding sexual activity because of poor body image deprives you of the opportunity to discover that a partner can enjoy you sexually just the way you are. Then you don't get some positive experiences to counteract your perception that you don't look good enough to enjoy sex.

A third issue is the physical problems that often come with growing older, such as high blood pressure, diabetes, back problems, joint pains, and other ailments associated with aging. Anything that makes you feel physically uncomfortable is likely to distract you from sexual interest. Furthermore, many of the medications used to treat some of these problems have a numbing effect, which also decreases sexual pleasure. Focusing on the aches and pains associated with aging pulls attention away from more pleasurable and lively sexual feelings. The more I'm thinking about how my back hurts, the less I'm thinking about how good other parts of my body feel. And if I'm caught up comparing how I'm less flexible now than I was in my thirties, I'm less present in the moment, more preoccupied with the past. I'm thinking about what's wrong with me, not what's right with this experience.

When they first met online, Dee, age forty-eight, lived in the Midwest, and Rachel, who was fifty-one, lived in New England. After several weeks of emailing and telephone calls, they arranged a rendezvous. Both were impressed, and they fell in love with each other. In addition to their online and telephone contacts, they began meeting every other weekend, alternating visits between their homes. A year later, Rachel's company offered her an outstanding promotion if she would agree to transfer to another city. They decided that this was their opportunity to join their lives, so Dee moved with her, and they began living together in their new home, in a new city.

"At first," Dee said, "it was wonderful to finally be together every day. We were excited about being a couple, having a home together, and establishing our new social network together instead of having such separate lifestyles. But then, it started getting harder . . . and then we stopped having sex. I want to, but Rachel says she doesn't feel like it. She thinks she's menopausal."

Rachel wasn't as happy with her new position as she had hoped to be. It was a step up in terms of management, but also in terms of stress and demands. She felt tired, disappointed, and preoccupied. Rachel also had some irregularities in her menstrual cycle, felt very disinterested in sex, and gained about twenty pounds in the past year. She wondered if

>

hormonal changes could explain how she felt. When she talked to Dee about her lack of sexual interest, Rachel usually said, "It's not you, it's me. I think I'm depressed, and my hormones are changing." Dee wanted to be supportive but felt hurt and deprived. She understood that Rachel wasn't feeling good and believed that hormones could have a significant impact on desire, but she missed their sexual intimacy. As she said, "I'm not crazy about my job either, but it would help me if we felt closer. . . . And doesn't menopause go on for years? How long do we have to wait?"

It was interesting that Dee and Rachel focused on a physiological explanation for loss of sexual interest without taking into account their many environmental transitions: from living separately to living together, from home turf to a new city, and from an active social network to no network at all. Additionally, Rachel's job transition had been rough. Instead of feeling capable and confident at work, she felt disoriented and insecure. Dee's work situation was less negative, but otherwise, she was experiencing similar stressors. All of this was reduced to a single physiological explanation for their decreased sex life. Meanwhile, their coping styles seemed very different.

Dee coped by turning toward Rachel. When she felt lonely or displaced, she longed for Rachel to hold her. She focused her energy on their relationship and thought about ways to bring them closer. Sexual intimacy gave her not just pleasure but comfort. It helped her feel connected, reminded her of their special attraction to each other, and reassured her that "We can do this together!" For Dee, more emotional and sexual contact would have helped solve the problems of all their recent environmental changes. She kept turning toward Rachel for that solution and feeling rebuffed. Unfortunately, the rejection just made Dee feel more needy and fueled her efforts to pursue Rachel more vigorously.

In contrast, Rachel's energy was focused internally. Her increased eating may have been an effort to comfort herself, but it resulted in feelings of shame around her weight gain and made her more reluctant to expose her body in sexual situations. Rachel was also feeling some shame at her job, as she perceived that she wasn't doing as well as she'd hoped. She began withdrawing more and more, hiding her feelings and focusing on unpleasant body sensations: feeling bloated, tired, uncomfortable, and other sensations easily labeled as "menopausal." Rachel's hiding solution wasn't helpful. In fact, it made the problem worse, because she cut off opportunities to hear the kinds of supportive and complimentary feedback that could have helped her feel better about herself. For example, because she felt "fat," she wouldn't give Dee a chance to show her how she appreciated and enjoyed her body. She wasn't talking with her old friends or new acquaintances about work stressors because she was afraid they'd think she was a failure. Her loss of support and feedback left Rachel feeling more depressed and isolated and less likely to venture into sexual territory with Rachel.

The other factor that was woven into Dee and Rachel's sexual dynamics was that they had never lived together before moving to this new city. In fact, most of their relationship had been online or on the telephone, and it's usually easier to maintain the early stages of falling in love and romantic fantasy when you're not actually *with* your partner that much. They encountered a huge reality check with each other at the same time they encountered a new city, new jobs, and new social networks. It would have been natural for one or both of them to feel a sudden drop in sexual interest at that time—but it could also have been frightening. "What have I done? Uprooted my life, given up my friends, moved off to this strange place—and now I don't even know if I want *you* that much!" This acute anxiety doesn't help a sexual relationship. Instead, it usually brings out some self-defeating coping styles: Rachel's withdrawal and Dee's pursuit.

For Dee and Rachel, relational and emotional factors were probably having more impact on their sex life than Rachel's hormones. Wrapping

>

up all these issues as "menopause" doesn't do justice to the complexities of the situation. Of course, there are real hormonal changes that happen: estrogen, progesterone, and testosterone levels can fluctuate and play havoc with your sense of well-being. We can explore these more specifically, but keep this in mind: The vast majority of middle-aged and older women say that your relationship with your partner, your physical health, and your emotional well-being affect your sex life more than your hormones.

In his Pulitzer Prize–winning book, *The Denial of Death*, Ernest Becker addresses the fundamental limit of human nature: the unavoidable fact that we all have to die.[2] According to Becker, we don't take life seriously enough because we don't want to admit that it has to end. We're not motivated to seize the day if we tell ourselves there will be lots of other days. We miss "once in a lifetime" opportunities by denying that a lifetime is limited, or say, "I'll decide that tomorrow" without acknowledging that tomorrow may not happen. We pretend we can live forever through legacies, children, facelifts, or even red sports cars. These distractions soothe fears of death temporarily, but in the end, there's still an end. Dancing around that inevitability, Becker suggests, keeps us from living as fully as possible.

We're also afraid to live life to its fullest because the more we let ourselves be open to the experience of the present, the more loss we may feel when it passes. We may recite "'tis better to have loved and lost than never to have loved at all," but sometimes we don't live that way. Fear about future losses can prevent us from being open to the experience of the present. But life really happens in the present. Being absorbed in the present is the best way to cope with fear of future loss. After all, losses are going to happen anyway. Better to face these with memories of full experiences instead of regrets about missed opportunities.

It takes courage to continue loving as deeply as you can in the face of an eventual, certain ending. Sex therapist David Schnarch suggests that disengaging sexually is a way to protect yourself from this pain—to control loss by inducing it.[3] And it's usually not even a conscious decision to induce this loss. Sometimes women forsake their sex lives at the first sign of their diminishment—even though fluctuations in desire are normal and occur throughout life, and even though there are many ways to prolong the lifespan of your desire. Unfortunately, too many women unwittingly create premature endings due to misguided and limiting beliefs about aging.

At the beginning of each workshop or professional conference I hold, I ask participants to complete a questionnaire based on the statements about female sexuality found in chapter 1. Almost everyone agrees with the statements "For women, sexual interest tends to decline with age" and "Hormonal fluctuations are the greatest cause of changes in women's desire levels." Unfortunately, these limiting beliefs are deeply engrained. That's why, even though they aren't really true, these can become self-fulfilling prophecies. A woman who believes that hormones rule her sex life may take little or no action to make the kinds of changes that might enhance her sexual feelings as she grows older, and then, when she starts to feel a decline in desire, she might attribute it to hormones and leave it at that. The pseudo-explanations of hormones leave women feeling resigned about their sexuality or searching for solutions that are usually nonproductive. For example, I've heard very detailed explanations of complicated neuropathic "treatments" based on the premise that tinkering with hormones is the single best approach to enhancing sexual desire. This premise is contradicted by much of the research on female sexuality.

A realistic look at the data helps broaden the picture of sexuality and aging, as well as our understanding of what "sexual desire" really means. In chapter 1, I mention the Laumann surveys of 1993 and 2005. In those surveys, a lack of sexual desire was reported by more *younger* women than older women: 32 percent of women in their twenties, and 27 percent of women in their fifties, met the criteria set by the researchers for the diagnosis of "low sexual desire."[4] There are also many other research studies showing that younger women are more likely to report less sexual desire and satisfaction.[5]

In one therapy group, a woman named Anne, who had just turned sixty, said "I feel ashamed." Her honesty was poignant, as she talked about ways she felt vulnerable and exposed. She was older than most of the people she worked with, and she worried that they thought she was out of sync. But she especially worried that they thought she looked old. Anne had been a striking young woman and was used to getting a lot of attention. Now she interpreted the looks differently. She was afraid people were feeling sorry for her because of her gray hair and wrinkled skin. She was seven years older than her partner and wondered if Penny secretly wanted to be with someone younger.

As Anne talked about her feelings of shame about aging, she got a lot of support from other women in the group. The ones who were her age understood exactly what she meant and told her they appreciated her for saying it out loud. This made it easier for them to talk about their own shame about aging. The women who were younger than Anne expressed surprise. It hadn't occurred to them that Anne would feel ashamed of her age. They saw her as a very good-looking woman and assumed that she felt confident about her appearance. Anne's honesty was a reminder of how vulnerable and self-conscious we can be underneath whatever surfaces we present to others. One woman said, "I feel more compassion for all of us, knowing how much we women judge ourselves about our looks."

Nothing decreases shame like talking about it with others who are supportive and nonjudgmental. It's like exposing something that's been locked up in a dark closet to sunshine and fresh air—it feels less loaded and scary. You can see people's faces as you talk about your "secret shame," and you'll notice that they don't look critical or disdainful. Instead, they usually look understanding and may be nodding in agreement because they know how you feel. Then your private pain becomes a universal experience that others can help you tolerate and even overcome. And even if they don't share exactly the same concerns, almost every human being has moments of feeling embarrassed about something. Knowing this helps ease the shame and transform it into compassionate understanding. This is what happened for Anne as she talked more about her age in this very empathetic group of women.

After feeling some emotional release, Anne was able to appreciate another aspect of herself, which was how much she enjoyed being active and engaged. In some ways, she said, she felt even more pleasure in what she *did* and less pleasure in how she looked. The trade-off seemed to work for her, but only after she had a chance to work through the feelings of loss and shame related to aging.

Furthermore, a survey conducted by the American Association of Retired Persons (AARP) in 1999 revealed that 85 percent of married women in their sixties and 25 percent in their eighties were still sexually active [6] These women said they believed that sexual interest and activity continues well into old age if you are healthy. Only 35 percent of these women said their sexual interest had decreased from what it was in their younger years This is consistent with my clinical experience, in which the level of interest in sex seems fairly stable over time, with minor fluctuations due to specific circumstances, such as an illness or a relationship conflict.

Often, women are surprised to hear these data . . . until they think more carefully about their own sexual histories. Then they smile, recalling how they enjoyed sex more as they gained more experience, got to know their bodies better, and became more comfortable expressing their preferences. Their self-awareness and improved communication skills combine to help them enjoy more sexual satisfaction as they get older. In the follow-up interviews that were part of my 2007 survey of lesbian sexual behavior,[7] and also in my therapy sessions, I've talked with a number of women who are over fifty and sexually active with a partner. One paradox emerged from these talks. Many of these women said their sexual feelings aren't as physically intense as they used to be, but that they enjoy sex as much or *more* than they did when they were younger. Several of them said they like the way that sexual intimacy provides a unique emotional and physical connection with a partner, and that they feel more confident about arousal and orgasm than they used to because they know their bodies very well. Most said that the loss of physical intensity is outweighed by the emotional gains and satisfaction they feel about still being sexually active.

What older people enjoy most about sex seems to have more to do with emotional and spiritual dimensions than simply physical pleasure, although that's nice too. When I recently asked my colleague, marriage and family therapist Ann Walter, about her thoughts on sexuality and aging, she focused on the spiritual dimensions. "An orgasm can be more than physical excitement and release," she said. "It can bring moments of transcending boundaries, of getting outside ourselves and merging, temporarily, with another, and even with a universal Spirit." Sexual intimacy provides a unique opportunity to connect with our own bodies and with the universal essence in each other. Your orgasmic bliss is unique to you, and to me too, and knowing this lets us temporarily erase a boundary between us. Connecting with something greater than ourselves adds a spiritual dimension to the physical pleasures of sexual intimacy.

The pharmaceutical industry has strong financial incentives to make us believe our sexuality depends entirely on chemical solutions. After all, there's a lucrative market for pills, not for positive behaviors that enhance sexuality at all ages. According to the psychologist and researcher Julia Heiman, director of the Kinsey Sex Research Institute, the major funding for studies of female sexuality comes from drug companies, which have poured money into research on pharmaceutical solutions, such as "the female Viagra," with no significant success. In contrast, the funding for behavioral research is almost nonexistent today.

Testosterone gets a lot of attention because of its very specific effect. It can stimulate libido very directly and rapidly. For example, some studies show that 65 percent of menopausal women with depleted testosterone who received supplementation experienced an increase in libido, sexual response, frequency of sexual activity, and increased sensitivity of erogenous zones.[8] Many women who use supplemental testosterone after surgical removal of the ovaries experience a restoration of sexual feelings rather quickly. In fact, if it weren't for the side effect of developing male secondary sexual features, such as extra hair growth and a deeper voice, many more women would probably love testosterone supplements.

The current fascination with testosterone belies the fact that, according to the author and physician Christiane Northrup, testosterone levels do *not* fall significantly after menopause.[9] The vaunted testosterone decline is actually very gradual, beginning in the late twenties and continuing through midlife. According to Northrup, this decline may actually stop before menopause. In other words, while there is plenty of evidence that very low levels can suppress sexual desire, there's no evidence that these levels are lower after menopause.

Randi and Joanne were both in their early forties and had been together for ten years. They were a cute, friendly couple who talked openly about their issues. They came to therapy because they were having more fights, fewer good conversations, and no sex for the past year. Both Randi and Joanne said they knew they loved each other, but they worried that the

>

constant conflict and lack of sexual intimacy was going to destroy their relationship.

Their sexual history together was fairly typical for lesbian couples. After an initial few months of having sex once or twice a week, they gradually drifted into a pattern of having sex monthly, then a few times a year, then not at all. Because Joanne had always been more interested in sex, she did most of the sexual initiation. For a long time, Randi went along, reluctantly. But in the past year, Joanne started to feel resentful about always having to initiate. So she stopped. And Randi seemed fine with no sex at all.

Joanne was very worried about their lack of sexual connection and felt a lot of pain and fear about sexual rejection. In her twenties, she discovered that her then-husband—who had stopped wanting to have sex with her—was having an affair. Joanne was afraid that Randi's sexual withdrawal might be the beginning of the end.

Randi traced her lack of sexual desire to a complete hysterectomy, including loss of ovaries, when she was thirty-two. Prior to her hysterectomy, Randi said, she was a different person sexually—"a real Casanova." "When I was younger," she said, "I could walk into a bar, pick out who I wanted to go home with, and make it happen." Apparently, this happened frequently. Randi said women were very complimentary about her skills as a lover, and this was a real boost to her self-esteem. "The hysterectomy really changed me," she said, sadly. "I don't feel like the same person." She had tried hormone replacement but felt it didn't make much of a difference.

At this point, Joanne gently interjected. "But you stopped being interested in sex *before* your hysterectomy."

Randi looked a little startled but then agreed. After more consideration, she realized that she began feeling less sexual desire just a few months after she and Joanne began living together. Randi also acknowledged that none of the relationships from her "Casanova" days had lasted more than a few weeks, except for one six-year relationship, in which she

>

also lost interest in sex after a few months. Clearly, her lack of desire was not just about hormones.

I assured Randi that I completely believed her about the impact of her hysterectomy. Many women who have radical hysterectomies report the same feelings: a loss of sexual desire, difficulty getting aroused or having an orgasm, even a loss of aggressive feelings in general. Randi had experienced real losses and had every right to be sad about them. But that wasn't the whole story.

As we talked more, other important themes affecting their lack of sexual connection started to come up. Randi obviously missed her younger, more butch self: aggressive, confident, unfettered. She had greatly enjoyed her years of dating and sexual freedom—especially the thrill of flirting and seduction. Randi had assumed she felt so sexual in her "glory days" because she had all her testosterone available. She had not thought about her dating days as high-foreplay, low-demand situations—but that's what they were. All that flirtatious behavior was a way she kept turning herself on, and she enjoyed the rush of novelty, repeatedly. It simply wasn't compatible with *sustaining* sexual intimacy in an ongoing relationship, like the one she had with Joanne.

By focusing on hormones as an explanation for her low desire, Randi had also been avoiding a sensitive topic: She had always wanted Joanne to be more expressive and communicative in bed. Even though Joanne was obviously very interested in sex, she was very quiet during lovemaking. Unfortunately, in the past, when Randi tried to ask Joanne for what she wanted, Joanne felt Randi came off sounding patronizing and superior.

Joanne resented Randi's superior tone, but she seemed to feel inferior without Randi's help anyway. Joanne sounded apologetic and embarrassed when she talked about her family and upbringing. She was one of five children, raised in a lower-middle-class family with alcoholic parents and grandparents whom she loved but was ashamed of. She also seemed

>

to feel very responsible for them, and it was very hard for her to set any limits with them.

It was interesting to see how their different personalities had contributed to the demise of their sexual relationship. Randi, an externalizer, had been quick to attribute her loss of desire to hormones, for which she had no responsibility or control. When she was reminded that her loss of desire happened before the loss of hormones, she quickly shifted to blaming Joanne for being too quiet in bed. For her part, Joanne, an internalizer, had been reluctant to confront Randi's "hormone hypothesis," even though she knew it wasn't accurate. She was also quick to accept blame for being too quiet, forgetting that she had been the one initiating sex for years.

As these two women began to talk openly about their sexual concerns, it became obvious that the focus on Randi's hormones had prevented them from addressing a workable problem. Randi could look for ways to bring her Casanova self into their bedroom, and Joanne could learn ways to show more sexual responsiveness. Habitual patterns of blame and shame can be changed, once they become obvious and explicit. And yes, hormones make a difference—but not nearly as much as being honest and deliberate about preserving sexual intimacy.

Northrup does recommend that women who are experiencing a notable decline in libido get their unbound (free) testosterone and dehydroepiandrosterone (DHEA) levels checked. DHEA is the main ingredient from which the body manufactures testosterone. A physician can prescribe natural testosterone, which is available through a formulary pharmacy and comes in the form of capsules or vaginal creams. Another option is to take DHEA, which is available without a prescription at most health-food stores, at a dose of 5 mg to 10 mg once or twice a day. Northrup suggests that increases in DHEA may raise testosterone levels enough to improve libido. Of course, it is very important to talk with your doctor before taking these kinds of supplements, as there can be interactions with certain medical conditions or medications which could be potentially harmful.

Jen Johnsen, an internist and medical researcher, offers a balanced perspective on sex and hormones.[10] She recommends that doctors take a good medical history of women who wonder if their level of sexual desire is being negatively impacted by hormones. This history can help the doctor and patient to discern if sexual changes have been abrupt or gradual, and if there were any obvious physical or environmental precipitants. For example, a sudden loss of sexual feelings after a complete hysterectomy would certainly suggest plummeting testosterone, and your doctor might suggest options such as a testosterone patch or estrogen ring. In contrast, a gradual loss corresponding to an unhappy relationship suggests that interpersonal issues are at the core of the problem. In this case, relationship and sexual counseling would be a more appropriate treatment approach.

Reducing sexual desire to hormones oversimplifies complicated questions, with many implications. For example, Johnsen explained, the body has a way of balancing hormones by itself. Introducing supplemental testosterone could trigger estrogen production to slow down, much the way that increased heat will shut down the thermostat. Bringing in testosterone from the outside could stimulate the body to produce less from the inside. In the end, you could wind up with the same levels, just not from the same sources. Using supplements to override negative relationship factors could simply obscure or minimize problems that could be addressed more therapeutically. These are the kinds of issues that can be clarified by paying close attention to a sexual history.

Johnsen also talks about the importance of physical exercise. "Sex is a physical activity," she says. "It's active, and you need to participate." Regular exercise—at least twenty minutes, four times per week—builds strength and generates endorphins that make your body a happier place to be. You will appreciate the extra strength and muscle tone when you're engaged in the very physical act of making love. Most importantly, being physically active places you inside your body, enjoying how you *feel* instead of being outside, wondering how you *look*. Every serious article on sex and aging encourages exercise and physical activity to increase sensory awareness, decrease body image problems, and protect your overall health. Exercise seems to enliven the body and increase self-esteem. That's a great combination for sexual intimacy at any age.

It's normal for sexual needs to shift somewhat, and this doesn't mean what happened before was deficient. Rather, your body may have shifted a bit, and something different might feel better now. And if you're feeling insecure about how you look, an honest discussion may help you get out of your own negative self-judgment and into an empathic connection with another woman who probably knows how you feel.

After a lifetime of dealing with antigay discrimination, we can enjoy one special lesbian advantage: Because we're women, we typically live longer, and our partners live longer too. Those of us who are single have a larger potential partner pool as we grow older. Our odds of finding a partner are much better than those of older straight women, who outnumber their male peers more and more with every year they live. How delightful that our sexual orientation actually becomes an advantage in later life, and that we have an opportunity to be with a wonderful woman throughout our final days.

It may help to remember that you have to die anyway, whether you live fully or not. You might as well enjoy as much as you can, as long as you can. That's about more than just going out in a blaze of glory. It's about sharing your light with each other as long as you can. What's the alternative? Quit ahead of time? Or live as fully as possible, being active and engaged in life, in friendship and community, and in sexual intimacy?

Our challenge for our time is to debunk old myths about sex and aging. The biggest myth is that older women aren't interested in sex. Just ask them—they are! Hormones affect women of all ages, but they don't rule. Body image is an issue, but aging usually brings more acceptance and less superficiality. Physical ailments increase with old age, but so do the psychological and spiritual perspectives that enrich sexual experiences. Most of all, awareness of mortality brings gratitude for the richness of life, including the special pleasures of sexuality.

Your Turn

① What are your own negative stereotypes about sex and aging? Can you think about where you learned these and how much you really believe them to be true? Did any of the facts presented in this chapter surprise you? For example, had you assumed that young women have greater desire than older women? Think about the implications of finding out that isn't true, and how that might change the way you approach sexual opportunities.

② Can you think of any positive role models—older women who seem sexually vibrant to you? What would you guess their secret is? Think about some ways you can incorporate their "secret" into your own life. Pay special attention to some of their behaviors. For example, are they very physically active? Socially involved? Publicly affectionate with their partners? How often do you do these activities?

③ Are you feeling vulnerable and ashamed because you are aging? Are you as judgmental of others who are aging? Whenever you're dealing with an issue that makes you feel exposed and ashamed, check yourself for "projection." Projection is the process by which you project your feelings about yourself onto others and assume they are judging you in the same harsh light that you're shining on yourself. Instead of projecting, why not look around and see what other women look like? Some must look older than others, and some characteristics probably appeal to you more than others. What are the characteristics that you especially like about yourself?

④ Hormones and exercise can help sustain sexuality for individuals, but nothing helps with sexual intimacy more than clear, positive communication with your partner. It's important to talk with her honestly about any changes you've noticed in your own body. Do you need more-intense or less-intense stimulation? Do you need it to last longer? Do you need additional sources of stimulation, or lubrication? Do you enjoy sexual intimacy most when you're on vacation? Going to your weekend cabin? Waking up Sunday morning? Pay special attention to the things you avoid talking with her about—those are probably the most important ones.

⑤ Imagine that you knew you only had another year to live. How would you like to relate to your partner during that time? Would you want to withdraw to save her—and you—the pain of loss, or would you want to enjoy as much as you could together? What do you think you'd appreciate the most during that year? How can you use that knowledge now, even without a known date of departure?

7

Fidelity Issues

MONOGAMY IS STRAIGHTFORWARD: You have sex with only one person. But the concept of fidelity is much more nuanced and complicated. What defines "sex"? What's the difference between noticing someone is hot and lingering with long fantasies about being with her? How much of a transgression is it to kiss passionately, but do nothing else? Or to talk about wanting to kiss but not actually doing it? Or to have secret conversations that no one else knows about? Most importantly, do you and your partner have the same perspective on these questions? Do you both place the same value on your sexual intimacy with each other? Do you both agree how much sexual energy—if any—is okay to direct elsewhere?

Most dictionaries define "fidelity" as an adherence to promises, commitments, or obligations. In audio recording, however, "fidelity" refers to how accurately sounds and images are reproduced. Perhaps this is a more useful way to look at fidelity. How accurately does your behavior with other women reflect the tone and quality of your relationship? If your partner assumes that you are faithful to her, is that the signal that you are sending others? Couples who choose open or multiple-partner relationships can be faithful to each other if their behavior with others accurately reflects agreements they have with each other. On the other hand, it's also possible to be exclusively monogamous and emotionally unfaithful if your behavior with others doesn't reflect the words you and your partner have said to each other.

Probably because it is so devastating, it's hard to write a balanced discussion of infidelity. It'd be simple to just say, "All cheaters are horrible, selfish people," and leave it at that. And I'm sure plenty of people would be satisfied with that verdict. I do believe that honesty is the best policy, and I've rarely heard a completely sound "excuse" for being dishonest to a partner. But, for better or worse, things are usually not so cut and dried. Infidelity is very often the result of a complex situation between two people who love each other but have not been communicating well. The situation is complex, and so is the damage of infidelity. The residue of hurt, anger, betrayal, guilt, and shame can linger for years—or for a lifetime.

You're at a party with your partner when another woman starts talking to her. Your partner, who's been fairly quiet all night, begins laughing and looking at her with interest. The other woman moves a little closer, and their voice levels drop a notch. And then you feel that icky mix of feelings and thoughts—hurt, anger, fear, and humiliation—as you think, *She looks excited about her. She wants to be with her. She likes her more than me.* You begin to feel very small. You want to escape but can't bear to leave the two of them together. The thoughts and feelings channel into a burning sensation in the pit of your stomach. You're jealous.

I hope that you can find a way to soothe yourself so the jealousy doesn't eat you up. Some people can't. Jealousy can be an intense,

>

primitive feeling that drives people into doing really stupid things. But why is jealousy so powerful?

Evolutionary biologists believe that human jealousy originally functioned as a way to ensure propagation of the species by protecting primary relationships, in which children could be raised to adulthood. They say that it is a hardwired human emotion that evolved in order to signal a threat to the primary relationship. And in fact, brain scans show that jealousy activates the attachment system of the brain, a genetically ingrained circuit that is the foundation of our social bonds and that prompts widespread distress when threatened.[A] This would explain why jealousy provokes such strong feelings: At a core level, the threat to a primary social bond is life-threatening. We rely on each other for survival, and when we say, "I'd just die if I lost you," deep down inside, we take that literally, and may react with a "fight or flight" response. This is when the stupid things can happen. In court, they call them "crimes of passion," which is putting a positive spin on a destructive behavior. Whatever it's called, jealousy can stir up a lot of problems.

Jealousy can also stir up some personal growth, according to humanistic psychologist William Rock.[B] He suggests that jealousy forces us to grasp the difference between loving someone and trying to own her. According to Rock, loving is about appreciating, adoring, enjoying someone for who they are, not about trying to make them belong to you. He used the example of a flower. You can enjoy and appreciate a beautiful flower standing in its own spot in the garden—you can love it. But when you attempt to own it, you cut it, sever it from its natural habitat, take it home, and try to preserve it in a vase where it will eventually lose its life energy.

Rock claims that jealousy forces us to acknowledge some of our deepest fears: losing a loved one, losing self-esteem, and dissolving into oblivion, a là, "I'm nothing without you." Confronting those most basic

>

fears forces us to let go of possession and to experience real love, appreciating another for who she is, a là, "You're wonderful even without me." His ideal of pure love is inspiring, even for those of us who doubt that we mere mortals can achieve this level of generosity.

For those of us who can't be that magnanimous, what do we do with this toxic brew of thoughts and feelings? First, a little self-analysis is in order. Ask yourself, *What's the intensity and duration of this jealousy? Am I generally a jealous person, in every relationship I'm involved in? Or is there something particular about this relationship that makes me more vulnerable to feeling jealous?* It's important to honestly check yourself out on these questions. If you're always jealous, in every relationship, it's almost certainly something about *you,* and it would be in your best interest to understand yourself more. For one thing, extreme jealousy can limit your partner choices. Most healthy women view extreme jealousy as an effort to control and possess them, and they don't like it. You may find yourself getting rejected by the women you find most interesting. Your behavior may be working against your goals. Any time you become aware of being caught in a self-defeating cycle, it's worth it to take a hard look, perhaps with the help of a therapist, to help you get out of it. You have a lot to gain if you can let go of some of the jealousy and learn to risk loving without trying to control.

On the other hand, if this is an unusual feeling for you to have, it's important to look at the relationship and situation you're in. Ask yourself, *What led up to this attack of jealousy? What is it about this person or this situation that's stirring up these feelings? How have I been feeling about her lately? How have I been feeling about myself? Have I felt jealous with her before? What happened the last time? Was I mistaken, or was there really some other interest going on? What did I say to her? What did she say to me? Did that help me feel better?*

After all that self-analysis, you probably need to talk with your partner about your feelings. But only talk if you can talk in "I-statements"

>

(see chapter 9 for an explanation of I-statements). Maybe she'll say she enjoyed the attention she was getting elsewhere but really wants it from you, or that she understands why you felt jealous and would have felt the same way. Maybe this can lead you both into talking about some problems in your relationship.

Of course, it's hard to speak in perfect I-statements when you're hurting and scared—but it's really important to try. If you lapse into accusing and attacking, you'll push her away. She may lash back at you or simply withdraw and stop talking, and either way, you'll cheat yourself out of some valuable information.

What valuable information, you wonder? Your jealousy is telling you something, either about yourself or about your relationship. If it's about you, it will help you to know this so you can calm yourself down the next time it happens. You can remind yourself, *I felt this way before, and it turned out I was wrong; she wasn't interested in someone else, she was really loving and sweet to me when I talked to her about it.*

On the other hand, if you're jealous for reasons that make sense when you talk about it openly, you need to know what those reasons are. Is there something missing in your relationship? Are you involved with someone who likes to flirt a great deal? Is that going to be an ongoing problem for you? If so, better to address the issue as soon as you can, because it will only get worse.

I haven't said much about asking her to reassure you when you're jealous. That's okay to do occasionally, but asking for reassurance is a little too easy, and often, it doesn't really work. It's easy because then you don't do the hard work of self-examination, so you don't learn things about yourself that can help you feel less jealous in the future. And a lot of times, it doesn't work. Reassuring words can stick for a little while and then slip away. Then you ask for more reassurance, and at some point, your partner starts to get exasperated with you. So pay attention to how often you're

>

asking for that kind of reassurance, and ask yourself if you need to be doing more internal work to soothe these feelings.

Of course, there are times when words of reassurance are priceless. Your partner may be surprised to know you felt jealous, and eager to assure you that you're the one for her. She may appreciate you for being vulnerable about these feelings and draw closer to you. She may want to ease your worries, not because she feels controlled but because she loves you and wants you to know this. So yes, sometimes reassurance works like magic. Then you may even be grateful that jealousy helped get you there.

With all the damage that is done by infidelity, it's hard to fathom how anyone could be unfaithful to a loved one. And like most questions about human behavior, the answers are much more complex than they seem on the surface. For some, infidelity grows out of a long-standing estrangement that leaves a large space for someone else to fill. Sexual intimacy may have faded or ended altogether. The partners may try to convince themselves that sex isn't that important—until one of them feels attracted to someone else, and then sex becomes terribly important. Sometimes affairs are a way of acting out unspoken, simmering resentments, a way to punish a partner or demand her attention. During a crisis of personal confidence, an affair may offer an ego boost that restores shaky self-esteem.

The most common type of lesbian infidelity involves the "exit affair." For many women, an affair gives them the courage to leave an unsatisfying relationship. They may have outgrown the current relationship but fear moving on; they may be afraid they will regret leaving or hurt their partner and be seen as a villain. They may fear risking everything to try something new . . . so they take the "safe" route.

Only a minority of women who break this trust are simply "cheaters" who repeatedly have secret sexual liaisons but then return to an unsuspecting partner. Apart from such women, most of us are *not* calloused or insensitive to the emotional impact of our behavior. The person who was betrayed wonders how she can ever risk sexual vulnerability again, or trust her own judgment about potential partners. The unfaithful person knows, from her own behavior, that people can't always be trusted, that feelings and commitments can change very quickly. The "third party" knows that her new partner has been unfaithful before and may do it again, to her. All of the parties involved in an affair may come through the experience feeling more skeptical and guarded, less willing to be vulnerable, more burdened by negative emotions.

Despite the alarm and derision that are so often reserved for multiple-partner relationships, there are many people who enjoy loving, stable intimacy with two or more people. Although we lack good research data on this topic, my impression is that these kinds of relationships are slightly more prevalent today than in the past. In my own clinical experience, about fifteen percent of the women I've talked with say they've participated in sexual relationships with more than one partner. Of course, I don't know how many women choose not to share that information. It's

>

quite possible that the stigma about multiple-partner relationships keeps some women from talking about it.

People who write or speak positively about multiple-partner relationships emphasize the contrasts between traditional definitions and ideals: fidelity vs. monogamy, love vs. attachment, and jealousy vs. "compersion," a term frequently found in the literature meaning the joy or pleasure one takes in someone else's joy or pleasure.[c] While there are different models for alternatives to monogamy, all are characterized by an explicit agreement that people can have sex with more than one partner. People who participate in any kind of multiple-partner sexual relationships stress the importance of mutually agreeing to honor certain rules. The specifics of those rules tend to vary widely, as they are based on each individual's desires and boundaries, but some of the more general rules are standard enough to allow these types of relationships to be categorized as follows.

The most "casual" form is *swinging*, in which primary partners have casual sex with other couples, individuals, or groups. In this kind of recreational sex—sometimes called "sport sex"—the emphasis is on sexual pleasure, not emotional connectedness. People who want to participate in swinging often connect through online groups or clubs, which have varying degrees of control over the group membership. These groups have their own set of rules, particularly around the practice of safe sex, including use of condoms and avoiding certain higher-risk practices, such as penetration.

People in an *open relationship* are allowed to have sexual and romantic encounters outside the primary relationship. However, primary partners receive the most time, energy, and priority. In fact, they often live together and may have had a commitment ceremony or marriage. Secondary partners may also share some resources and life paths, but usually not on a daily basis, and usually much less so than primary partners.

>

People who are *polyamorous* are open to having honest, loving relationships with more than one person at a time. Though sex with more than one person is usually part of these relationships, the primary focus of polyamory is on love, not sex, guided by the principle that love knows no bounds, and that loving one person does not take away love for another. There is also usually a strong emphasis on honesty and truthfulness, though the logistics of managing polyamorous relationships vary from person to person.

Polyfidelity refers to a group in which all partners are primary to all other partners, and sexual fidelity is to the group. There is a shared intention of permanence with each other. More primary partners can be added, but only with everyone's consent. The bond is based on mutual and reciprocal love among all partners, not just sexual attraction or experimentation.

There are usually very positive motivations for practicing multiple-partner sexual relationships: commitment to each others well-being, sharing joy in each other's pleasure, and loving deeply without possessiveness. Perhaps people who hold these values deeply enough, and securely enough, can enjoy the unique benefits of nonmonogamous relationships. We simply don't have enough data to evaluate whether these relationships are more or less successful than monogamous ones. On the other hand, there's no shortage of opinions about this, mostly summarized by a friend's comment: "They don't work." Of course, many monogamous relationships don't work either, in the long run, so the question is still unanswered.

One thing that is obvious is that many efforts to challenge monogamy stem from negative motivations, and these are doomed to failure. Sometimes the motivation to "open up" a primary relationship is to make a partner jealous or to punish her for withholding sex. Another negative motivation can be the desire to please the partner who wants more freedom. Reluctant to say "no" for fear of losing their partner, some women

>

may try to force themselves into a torturous situation—one in which their very core values are being violated—so as to sustain a relationship that probably just needs to come to a close.

A thoughtful exploration of the ideals and practices involved in multiple-partner relationships is a good reminder of how much we can learn from alternative lifestyles and choices. Regardless of how many people we have sex with, any sexual relationship can be enriched if we remember to appreciate each other as separate, lovely beings—not just possessions that ease our insecurities about being alone. We benefit from staying in the present, being true to feelings instead of rules, being faithful and not simply monogamous. The joy of shared sexuality isn't necessarily restricted by certain boundaries.

For those who wish to explore multiple partner relationships, several books and websites are devoted to this specific topic. While having a primarily heterosexual focus, the website LovingMore.com offers articles, book references, and guidelines for successful navigation of these difficult waters. Other resources for gay men provide specific guidelines that are equally relevant for women. In *Open: Love, Sex, and Life in an Open Marriage* (Seal Press, 2008), author Jenny Block describes her own experiences as a woman who is married to a man and also pursues sexual relationships with women. Her perspectives may be controversial, but her warm, witty style makes this an interesting account of a polyamorous relationship.

According to psychologist and author Don-David Lusterman, a majority of heterosexual marriages survive infidelity.[1] However, he notes that the marriage is less likely to survive when the woman is the transgressor. One simple explanation for this is that men are less likely to forgive infidelity. However, other attributes of women's sexual experience may explain why most lesbian relationships don't seem to survive infidelity. Generally speaking, women seem less able to compartmentalize sex and more prone to develop an emotional attachment to a new sexual partner. This makes it harder for the involved partner to stop the affair, and for the discoverer to forgive. It could also be argued that women are less likely to cheat for purely sexual reasons, so when an infidelity occurs, it may indicate the primary relationship is already almost over. We're all familiar with the concept of serial monogamy, and affairs are often the links in the series. An astonishing number of women go directly from one relationship into another, even though they know that they should take a break between relationships, give themselves time to heal, and clear out some emotional baggage. In my clinical experience, 90 percent of the time, at least one person has already begun another emotional/sexual relationship before there is an actual physical separation from the first partner.

Our culture puts tremendous pressure on women to try to stay and work things out in a long-term relationship, often valuing commitment over happiness. However, there's something to be said for being able to let go and try again. Most women I've talked with who ended a relationship—often through an exit affair—say they have been happier since leaving. They may regret how they handled the break-up, and feel sad about the emotional turmoil they both felt and caused someone else, but in the end, they are glad they made the decision. Very often they say that the support of a new lover is what gave them courage to make the transition. Not admirable, perhaps, but it's very human.

Discovering that a partner has been unfaithful is painful and traumatic. Nothing stings like the image of a partner making love with someone else, knowing she wants, or at least wanted, someone more than you. It can wreak havoc on your self-esteem, and if the discovery comes as a complete surprise, it can throw a wrench into your trust of your own perceptions, which is very debilitating. It can make you question the foundation and meaning of your whole relationship. You may wonder how long it was going on, how you could have missed the signs. You may start to question your judgment, your attractiveness, your dispensability. You may wonder whether you were the last one to know, or whether your friends are feeling sorry for you. You may feel shame and rage, and you may even have suicidal or homicidal thoughts. Many people who go through this need to do a lot of work to make sure the betrayal doesn't become an obstacle in their ongoing ability to trust.

Before Debbie and John got married, they discussed their feelings about monogamy. Both of them believed that traditional marriage was based on patriarchal, oppressive constraints that interfere with individual freedom. Debbie identified as bisexual, because she felt strong sexual and emotional attraction to both men and women. For her, promising to only be sexual with her husband would be omitting an important part of her sexuality, as she wanted to remain open to the possibility of loving another woman as well. For John, promising to have sex only with Debbie was too limiting. Because of their shared values and trust of each other, they agreed to an open marriage. For several years, each of them occasionally had sexual encounters with others, but they always respected each other as primary partners.

>

Then Katie came into their lives. She and Debbie fell in love, and they began a sexual relationship. They also spent a lot of time with John, and gradually, Katie developed loving feelings for him too. They talked about these feelings and then began to include John in their lovemaking. Sometimes these were threesomes, sometimes different pairs: Debbie and John, Debbie and Katie, Katie and John.

After two years, Katie moved in with them. For several years, their understanding was that the three of them would be primary to each other, and that all members were also free to have secondary relationships with other partners. At different times, each of them had a sexual relationship with someone outside the group. But after several years of this, the three of them gradually came to the realization that outside relationships created additional turmoil that none of them wanted to deal with. For one thing, the new "outsider" often started a relationship saying she understood their arrangement, but later seemed to feel hurt or angry about not having equal status in the primary commitment they had with each other. At times Debbie or Katie or John would feel pulled into taking sides with a new partner and would turn against the others. After this happened a few times, the three had some long talks about their arrangement and how it was affecting each of them. They acknowledged that the costs of including others were outweighing the benefits. The three reaffirmed their commitment to each other and agreed to stop having any outside relationships. They have continued in a faithful relationship to each other for over thirty years. They are a wonderful, albeit rare, example of successful polyfidelity.

Debbie explained her viewpoint on the difference between fidelity and monogamy. "Monogamy is about promising not to have sex with anyone except your primary partner, but fidelity is about being committed to each other's well-being and to the well-being of the relationship. Sure, you can try to enforce a rule about who you can have sex with, but

>

you can't make someone put your feelings first or look out for your best interests. If two people both really value the freedom to have other sexual relationships, they can have other partners but remain faithful to each other. Like for us, I feel very secure knowing that both Katie and John really care about my well-being; that they'll do whatever they can to support me in my own growth and in our growth together. That's the most important thing to me."

Debbie's perspective, though challenging for most of us, brings up an interesting point. Most of feel that monogamy is the only way to ensure that we can trust our partners. But trust them to do what? Be there for us? Put us first? Let us lean on them when we need to? Look out for our best interests? That's the end result we really want . . . and monogamy certainly does not guarantee that. I for one have experienced monogamy without the joy and security of really trusting my partner to care about my feelings, to advocate for me, or to protect me when I need it. Whether or not we ever choose to enter into a multiple-partner relationship, we could probably all benefit from considering Debbie's point and asking ourselves whether what we really want is monogamy or fidelity.

Although it's no comparison to the feeling of being cheated on, being the one who was unfaithful is no picnic either. The guilt and the inner conflict between ethical values and intense emotions can be horrible. (To make matters worse, that emotional turmoil and secretiveness can add thrills to the affair, intensifying passion, which then feels too good to give up.) Often, the fear of the consequences is so intense that women never confess, which means they never really process the context of the affair enough to work through the issues that were involved. Instead, they continue on with the old relationship—or attempt to start a relationship with the new lover—without ever gaining an understanding of what led up to the infidelity. Not surprisingly, those unresolved issues have a way of lurking beneath the surface and manifesting, again and again, until they are dealt with.

Infidelity is an intense subject. Chances are that if you're reading this chapter, you are already sensing a feeling of sadness, anger, or guilt about a past infidelity. And even if you're secure in your current relationship, we can all summon fears of such a thing. Just the idea of being betrayed by the person we love most—the person we are most intimate with—is enough to fill us with jealousy, to turn our stomachs, and to make us anxious.

And for women in same-sex relationships, that kind of betrayal is even harder. We're already vulnerable in a world that disapproves of our sexual orientation. We need to trust our partners to stand with us, and we need to trust our friends to support us . . . and that makes it doubly hard when a partner cheats on us with a trusted friend, as is sometimes the case.

Rita and Marie had shared thirteen years together. Both were devout Catholics, both worked in hospital administration, and neither had ever been with anyone else. In the beginning, they were incredibly happy to have found each other. They bought a home together, went to Mass together, and even worked together . . . though they were very careful to hide their relationship, portraying themselves as good friends and roommates to the outside world.

>

Rita and Marie were both practical, hard-working women, and though they rarely argued, neither was very comfortable talking about emotional issues. They each were the type to assume "Things will work themselves out." In that sense, they easily navigated the little bumps and turns that take place in every relationship.

But things started to feel very different when Marie went to work for a national hospital consortium, taking a position that involved more money and more traveling. Rita was proud of her but also felt threatened and sometimes lonely. During that time, she discovered Dignity, a support group for gay Catholics. It was there that she met Angie, whom she quickly befriended. She was very pleased when Angie accepted an invitation to dinner at their home, and she was delighted to be able to introduce her to Marie. The three of them became close friends. They enjoyed Angie's company, and it meant a lot to both of them that Angie shared their Catholic and lesbian values. She became a regular dinner guest.

One night, Rita was delayed at work, and when she got home, she noticed that Marie and Angie seemed uncomfortable and that the cushions on the sofa seemed displaced. She was puzzled but couldn't think clearly, and she went back into the kitchen to get steaks ready to grill.

The next week Marie told Rita they needed to talk. With many tears and abject apologies, Marie confessed that she and Angie had begun a romantic relationship. She said she never intended for this to happen, but now that it had, she had to move on. Marie planned to move out soon and told Rita she wanted to divide up all their joint property and make a "clean break." And that's what she did. Within two months, Marie was gone, finances were settled, and Rita was living on her own for the first time in her life. She had lost her partner, her friend, and her spiritual support group. She had just turned fifty.

Rita's sense of safety and self-esteem was pulverized. She had brief flashes of rage and lengthy thoughts about suicide. She continued going

>

to work in the mornings, but usually came right home and spent her evenings with cocktails and ruminations.

A huge added blow for Rita was that Marie's affair was with someone she had met in Dignity. This was an affront to Rita's core beliefs in a loving God and a trustworthy spiritual community. The meetings with Dignity had been the first times in her life when she felt affirmed as a child of God and as a lesbian at the same time. They had helped her work through more layers of self-acceptance about her sexual orientation and given her a sense of meaning. Now it all seemed to be a shattered illusion.

It took Rita several years to get back on her feet emotionally. She started going to therapy, decreased her drinking, and began taking antidepressants. Gradually she began to reach out socially, although she was extremely sensitive to any perceived rejection. She had a few brief relationships with women who complained that she was emotionally detached and guarded. Rita agreed, but she liked it that way. Eventually, she found someone she liked enough to consider living with, someone who seemed a little insecure and who would probably never leave her. She knew she was settling, but she couldn't imagine letting herself really fall in love again.

Marie was a warm, sensitive woman who wept while she talked about what happened. Growing up, she had a fairly provincial and conservative background and she was used to being very discreet, even secretive, about her personal life with Rita. Once she started traveling for her new job, however, she started meeting colleagues who were openly gay. This was a huge breath of fresh air, but also disconcerting. She hadn't realized how much she had censored her life with Rita until she met other people who were more open. Marie felt herself, and her world, expanding. She was troubled by thoughts that crept in, questions of, *Would I still choose Rita now?* She was also troubled by the fact that Rita seemed to depend on her for everything. It felt like too much. Ironically, the Dignity group that gave

>

Rita so much support and validation also gave Marie some permission to detach. She wanted Rita to have other people to talk to and hoped it would help her be more independent. She thought it would help them expand their circle of friends, and made her feel less guilty about going off to explore new social outlets on her own. She didn't anticipate falling in love with someone in Rita's Dignity group.

When she did, Marie was stunned by the intensity of her passionate feelings. Her early sexual relationship with Rita had felt tender and good, but also reserved and sometimes awkward. Both of them had been young and sexually inexperienced, and neither of them had been comfortable talking about sex. They didn't communicate any particular likes or dislikes, or put their feelings into words with each other. Over the years their frequency of lovemaking had dwindled to once every few months. Marie assumed that this was just the natural progression of events for long-term couples. She felt guilty about hurting Rita, afraid of retaliation, and ashamed of being unfaithful, but she didn't want to give up what she had found. She felt like she'd fallen into a fountain of fresh water and was soaking in sensations she'd never had before. She said, "I hadn't known what I was missing, but when I did, I couldn't walk away from it."

Marie's guilt was heavy baggage that she took into her relationship with Angie. After she was finished with the logistics of separating, the emotional toll caught up with her. She and Angie struggled to build their own relationship but couldn't reach an untroubled place together. They parted amicably after a year. Marie admitted that she would always feel some guilt about what she did, but she knew for sure that her life had changed for the better since she left Rita.

With the benefit of time and hindsight, both Rita and Marie understood that more communication would have helped them in every way. If they had been able to talk about sex more openly, they could have enjoyed their intimate time together more. This would have strengthened their

>

positive feelings about loving another woman and decreased some of the homophobia that seemed close to the surface for both of them. The enhanced self-esteem that often accompanies sexual satisfaction could have helped them be more open about their relationship. Marie may have felt freer to be herself, and Rita may have felt stronger to stand on her own two feet. Most importantly, if they could have talked more openly, they could have discovered the deeper levels in each other and in themselves.

So much is riding on our trust of our partners. We face adversity for being lesbian, yet we feel validated and reassured in our identity by knowing that loving another woman feels right and natural. But that reassurance and sense of validation comes at a price. Many of us have lost friends and family because of our sexual orientation. Many of us have faced discrimination and have had to make sacrifices. On the other hand, women who have not come out but have rather been fairly closeted for years may be heavily dependent on each other, which means they can find themselves in a terribly lonely predicament when infidelity occurs.

All of this extra baggage creates a lot of weight, and our relationships must bear that weight. And if they cannot, the rupture can be crippling. As one of my clients once said, "I gave up my family for her, built my life around her, but it was all worth it, because I loved her so much. I used to feel so safe when she held me. But now she's holding someone else. How could she do that to me?"

If a couple does want to survive a powerful breach of trust such as infidelity, they must work hard and carefully to repair the damage done. Whether the relationship survives or not, both people need to do some personal investigation to understand what led up to the problem and how to avoid it in the future.

Both partners will need to talk about what was happening in their relationship that made them vulnerable to infidelity—but regardless of what led up to it, it is essential for the unfaithful partner to take full responsibility for her behavior. An attitude of "I said I was sorry, now let's move on" isn't going to work. She needs to spend a long time listening to how her actions affected her partner, validating those feelings, and expressing empathy and remorse. She also needs to offer to do whatever it takes to help her partner feel secure again: not seeing the other woman, not communicating with her, being transparent about where she is going and who she is with. She needs to keep asking her partner what she can do to regain her trust—and she needs to accept that this will take a long time.

Amanda and Elaine had lived together for eight years, owned a home together, attended each other's family functions, and presented themselves as "married" as much as a same-sex couple could. During their eight years together, Amanda had four affairs, each one lasting several months. Elaine didn't know about any of them.

With each affair, Amanda wondered if she would end up leaving Elaine for the new woman. She would fall passionately in love, feel crazy with sexual desire, and get caught up in fantasies about a new life with the new woman. But after the first flush faded, she'd realize that the new person couldn't really offer her enough to compete with what she had with Elaine. She would begin to pull back subtly, which would make the new woman feel wildly insecure and demanding of reassurances. Amanda

>

138

would then get annoyed by this apparent neediness, which she would use as justification to end the affair. She would go back into her safe world with Elaine, feeling slightly guilty but also content to pick up her old routines. She told herself that she and Elaine were meant to be together, that what Elaine didn't know didn't hurt her, and that the other women must have known it wouldn't have worked out because Amanda wasn't single.

Sometime after the fourth affair, Amanda recognized another aspect of this pattern. Years before, she had started a degree in physical therapy but never completed it. She worked as an assistant in a physical therapy clinic and envied the professional staff. She felt inferior at work and occasionally would have thoughts of going back to school to finish her degree. Instead, she would get distracted by a new infatuation. When she seduced a new partner, she felt a rush of self-esteem that temporarily overrode her feelings of inferiority at work. And when the affair ended, she would find herself once again considering her professional development.

Once she recognized this pattern, and how she was subconsciously holding herself back by indulging in these affairs, Amanda decided to enroll in school, and this time, stick it out. Unfortunately, this was the point when Elaine told her she had fallen in love with someone else. Elaine moved out, leaving Amanda stunned and struggling. But soon, Amanda started a new relationship, moved in with the woman, and never did make it back to school.

I felt sad that Amanda didn't explore her cheating behavior sooner. She might have seen how she was using affairs to avoid dealing with her achievement and self-worth issues. Seeking validation in the short-term reinforcement of a sexual conquest, she missed out on what she really needed, which was validation of her competency and power to take better care of herself. Like many women, she had been so conditioned to focus on being attractive enough for others that she didn't focus enough on her own aptitudes. Short-term gratification cheated her out of long-term satisfaction.

The partner who has been betrayed also has hard work to do. She needs to be willing to hang in there, to express both the angry and the hurt feelings, to ask whatever questions she has to ask in order to understand how this happened. At some point, after she has had plenty of time to process her own feelings, she needs to decide how much she wants to save this relationship. She will need to decide if she is able to try to trust again, or if she will stay stuck in bitter resentment about what has happened. If and when she decides to try again, then she can join in exploring the patterns of the relationship that may have contributed to infidelity. But if the hurt is too deep, she needs to have the courage to end the relationship. At the very least, she will respect herself for having made the effort, and the painful lessons learned will help her in future relationships.

The best time to start thinking about fidelity is in the beginning of a relationship. Granted, that's easier said than done. When you're falling in love, it can be difficult to pull back and be objective about what's happening. But no matter how great your passion, it's something everyone should attempt to do. Psychologists try to take a good relationship history with new clients—and you should do it with a new lover. History is a great predictor of future behavior. It's true that sometimes people change, but often they don't really change that much. If your new lover has a history of repeated affairs, think carefully about how that would feel if it happened to you. The repetition is problematic. If she had one affair, one time, listen to how she explains it. Does she take responsibility for it and tell you what she learned? Or does she seem to blame it on the other person or act like it was no big deal? How would you like to be that other person? I'm not recommending that you be judgmental about other people's behavior, but don't be naive, either. Instead, think carefully about how her attitudes would impact you if you were involved in an intimate relationship with her.

Tamara and Coretta had been together twelve years when the affair happened. Tamara was an optometrist who was very busy at work, but after hours, she could usually relax and focus on her passion, playing the clarinet in a community orchestra. Coretta was a college professor pursuing tenure, and her work never stopped. When she wasn't teaching, she was doing research, writing grants, and supervising students' projects. She spent most of her evenings and weekends immersed in reading and analyzing data. Coretta liked it when Tamara went to practice with her orchestra because it gave her more uninterrupted time to focus on her work. She told herself, and Tamara, that this workaholic behavior would be over as soon as she got tenure.

Meanwhile, Tamara was feeling lonely and began talking with one of the other musicians, a single woman named Celia. She enjoyed the rapport they had as musicians and began confiding in her about how distant she felt from Coretta. Celia was a warm and attentive listener who also happened to be a single lesbian. She invited Tamara to come over after orchestra practice, and their relationship evolved from there.

When they first slept together, Tamara was shocked with herself. She thought affairs were morally wrong and never thought she'd have one, yet there she was, in Celia's bed. She continued the affair for a few months but began to notice that she and Celia didn't have the kind of interesting conversations that she used to have with Coretta, conversations about intellectual interests, politics, or books they'd both read. Celia was caring and supportive, but beyond their shared musical

>

interest, the two didn't have much to talk about. When the initial sexual charge faded, Tamara ended the relationship with Celia. She also told Coretta about it.

Open communication saved their relationship: Coretta was angry and very hurt, and she expressed this to Tamara often, and at length, for several months. Tamara expressed remorse—and even more importantly, she stayed and listened. She told Coretta she would feel the same way, and would understand if she wanted to leave her—but she hoped she wouldn't. Instead, she hoped Coretta would forgive her and recommit to their relationship.

They went to couples' therapy and talked about the unfulfilled dreams that had been propelling both of them. To Coretta, getting tenure represented finally earning the approval of her high-achieving and critical parents and surpassing her sister, the "golden child" of the family. Tamara's dream was different. She felt complete and successful in her career and wanted someone to share the luxuries she had earned, take vacations with her, enjoy cultural events, even come to hear her play in the orchestra more often. She wanted more time with Coretta for the interesting conversations they had shared before Coretta began her single-minded pursuit of tenure. Analyzing what had gone wrong reminded both of them of what was right with each other, why they respected each other, and how they could work together to strengthen their bond.

Eight years later, these women are still together and are even more committed than they were before the affair. They are intentional in their intimacy, planning time to be together and being careful to talk about issues when they come up. Seeing them together is uplifting—they both express support and admiration for each other, touch each other affectionately and often, and ask each other interesting questions. They are also, to this day, very gentle with each other about the affair. They say that though it was painful, it turned their own relationship around. Tamara still

>

expressed remorse about her behavior, and Coretta took responsibility for her complete self-absorption during the tenure process. Both said the affair forced them to be more emotionally available to each other. It also helped when Coretta got tenure.

There are good reasons for almost any behavior when you understand the experiences that have shaped people. You can be empathic and compassionate about why some things happen and also be discerning enough to protect yourself from unwanted consequences. Most of us have the potential to act out sexually in ways that violate our own moral codes and our partners' feelings. We can be gentle about this potential in ourselves and in others, but we also need to be realistic.

While you're at it, do an honest reality check on yourself. If you've cheated, have you honestly and deeply examined your reasons? Do you just feel as if the devil made you do it, or do you blame it on your partner? There are many reasons relationships don't work out, but having an affair isn't the best way to try to exit or alleviate the problem. You'll sabotage your own future relationships, and risk hurting someone you love, if you don't make a long, hard, honest assessment of why you did what you did, who was hurt by that, and what you could have done differently. After examining your reasons, you may realize that you need to end your primary relationship. Telling someone you want to leave her may be painful, but it's less damaging to both of you than letting her find out you've already broken her trust.

For women who are tempted to be unfaithful, think hard about your motivations. Are you angry with your partner? Wanting to end the relationship? Feeling unattractive and unwanted? Wondering what else might be out there? Questioning your self-worth in some deep ways? It may be hard to resist the waves of passion you are feeling for a new woman, but giving in to these can wreak emotional havoc for all of you. And don't forget that the complicated and negative feelings most women have while having affairs often damage the new relationship in lasting ways. You may preserve a future love if you postpone acting on an immediate attraction.

When women have been betrayed in a sexual relationship, they need time to work through all the painful feelings. But sometimes they feel terribly clingy, with an almost urgent need to reassure themselves that they are desirable to someone else. This can present a dilemma. Trust takes time to build. There's just no way to know that you can rely on someone until you've had some time to rely on her. So this is the time to do a lot of talking with friends, loved ones, therapists—but not necessarily new lovers. No matter how much a new woman says, "You can trust me," the fact is, you can't trust anyone that quickly. Most of all, you need to trust yourself to be discerning, take slow steps, and see how you feel. It's great to go out and get feedback that you still look good, that other women find you attractive—but that's not going to fix the pain of betrayal. Compassion for yourself, and the courage to keep taking small risks, will carry you through this passage.

Sometimes it's very clear after infidelity that the relationship is over. But often, it's not. So how do you know when it's time to let go and when it's time to move on? A decision-making process called the Investment Model[2] can help analyze these questions. This requires evaluating what you have invested in the relationship, how much you still love the other person, and how likely it is that you will find someone you love more. If a one-time affair happened after twelve good years together and seemed related to a specific situational event, the relationship may be worth staying and fighting for. There would be a twelve-year investment, a reservoir of loving feelings from the good times, and a tangible explanation that could make sense to both partners. After twelve years together, you may feel sure that no one else is quite as good a match for you, and that she's worth the trouble of working through this. On the other hand, a series of affairs after a few years together doesn't bode well for long-term commitment.

One important difference between people is in how they attribute responsibility for adversity. Some people are called "internalizers," and others are "externalizers." These differences affect how they process affairs. An internalizer is only too willing to accept the blame for her partner's infidelity. If she has a problem, an internalizer assumes it is her fault and analyzes ways she should do things differently. This is often a good thing, but it can go too far. Often an internalizer takes responsibility for things that she had no control over. Then she falls into nonproductive self-blame and makes herself feel even worse.

Externalizers, on the other hand, have no such problem. They are quick to assume someone else is at fault and rarely acknowledge their own role in the problem. It's easy for them to see how others should change. They also are often completely lacking in any empathy for others' feelings and see themselves as special and entitled. Externalizers and internalizers often get together for a perfect fit—both can blame the internalizer for their mutual relationship problems. An unfaithful externalizer can easily blame her partner for being sexually unavailable. The internalizing partner will easily agree, and both conclude that it was mostly her fault. This sad arrangement can continue indefinitely unless the internalizer somehow learns that she deserves the same respect and power that her partner is claiming. She may learn this from friends, or from therapy, but she will need a lot of support to stop accepting responsibility for another person's behavior.

Most women who have experienced being on any side of an affair, and who have really thought about it, have a lot to say about honesty and deception. Deception undermines the trust that makes intimacy possible, and it shows up in many places. Infidelity is the big one, but smaller deceptions also erode the foundation of a relationship. Not telling a potential partner about previous infidelities is deceptive—that's information she should have, so she can make an informed decision about getting involved with you. Unexplained absences, undisclosed problems, unfulfilled promises—all of these are indicators of difficulty being authentic and vulnerable. This doesn't bode well for the kind of loving and trusting attachment most of us want.

Human attachment needs are rooted in dyads: An infant trusts her caretaker with her life, an adult trusts her partner with her heart. The greatest gift we can give each other is to create a safe space where we can risk being exposed, emotionally and sexually, knowing that our vulnerabilities will be handled lovingly and respectfully. We reveal ourselves in our most private places, both physically and emotionally. This is why fidelity is more than begrudging adherence to rules and promises. It's about dedicating ourselves to each other in a way that honors and protects both of us, and thereby lets us love more deeply.

Your Turn

① Think about your own history, or that of other women you have known who have ended a primary relationship with another woman. How often was there a third party involved? How did that seem to work out later? It's helpful to be realistic about what happens after an affair.

② What expectations do you and your partner have about fidelity? Is this a topic you can even discuss or is it too "unthinkable" to talk about? Can you discuss your limits on "innocent flirting," emotional connections with others, or overt attention to other women?

③ If your partner has been unfaithful, how are you deciding what to do? Could the Investment Model help you analyze what you've put in, how much you still love her, and how likely you are to find something better?

④ If you have been unfaithful, how are you handling it? Are you talking honestly about this with someone—your partner or a therapist, or both? Are you being honest about what led you into this? Are you taking responsibility for your part, or are you trying to blame others? Remember, it's in your best interest to understand yourself as much as possible, and that only happens when you're really honest about your role. This is what can help you have better relationships in the future.

⑤ If there's been infidelity in your relationship, are you talking about it constructively? Are you sharing your feelings or berating your partner? Are you willing to do what's needed to rebuild trust? Are you feeling like a victim, or can you feel empowered to take corrective action?

8

The Pressures of Parenthood

NOTHING CHANGES YOUR life like having a child. However it happens—childbirth, adoption, surrogacy, becoming a stepparent—the experience of nurturing and guiding a little human being can fill your heart, test your nerves, challenge your limits, and turn your world upside down. For many fortunate couples, the transition from childlessness to joint motherhood is an amazing time of deepening their communication, strengthening their bond, and enriching their love for each other as they share this wonderful and terrifying commitment to a new family. A shared desire to raise a child can bring out the very best in us, and many of us are eager to take on the challenge.

We may be eager, but few of us are ready. Unfortunately, this becomes obvious soon after the Blessed Event. Children are stressful! They are unbearably cute and precious beyond words, but they're also high-maintenance, relentlessly demanding little bundles of needs. The energy that's required to take care of them drains directly from the reservoir of your heart, and from your primary relationship.

For many couples, the arrival of a child signals the departure of their sexual bond. Research with heterosexual couples shows that there is a 70 percent decline in marital satisfaction the first year after the arrival of a child, and this decline is accompanied by a plunge in sexual activity.[1] Couples who previously made love several times a month say they may manage several times a year, if at all. Women who give birth biologically say they need time to recover from the physical trauma to their bodies and the psychological impact of converging sexual and reproductive functions. For some, it's difficult to associate that part of the body with sexual pleasure after going through the intense sensations and emotions of childbirth. For others, the pleasures and demands of motherhood make sexual needs a low priority.

Although no studies have been done specifically with lesbian couples, there's no reason to believe this would be different. In fact, my experience seems to confirm it: I've known about 80 or 90 lesbian couples who have given birth or adopted children. The vast majority say they stopped having sex immediately after the child arrived and rarely resumed any kind of regular or frequent sexual contact. In fact, about 80 percent of these couples are no longer together. And of the sexually active long-term couples (that happy 20 percent) I found in my 2007 survey, not one of them had any children in the home.[2] A few of the SA women did report having grown children who had already left the home, and two women who shared custody with an ex-spouse said they did enjoy sexual intimacy with their partners when the child was not there. In other words, it was the physical presence of a child in the home, not the fact of being a mother, that interfered with sexual intimacy.

The data certainly aren't encouraging—and yet, there are a few wonderful examples of couples who love their children and also love each other as sexual partners. When I've talked with these women, one theme stands out: good boundaries. To be more specific, they have what family therapists call "appropriate generational boundaries."[3] They meet their adult needs with adult partners and their mothering needs with their children. They understand that children are lucky to see their mothers protect their private time with each other. They model an intimate romantic bond that gives their children a secure foundation and a good example of adult intimacy. It's an amazing gift, and it's good for everyone in the family. It's another kind of loving loop: protecting your adult bond with your partner makes you a better partner and mother, which helps your child, which makes all of you happier.

Sounds good in theory, right? But what happens when "appropriate generational boundaries" collide with real life? What are the some of the reasons for the precipitous loss of sexuality among lesbian parents?

April and Jen had been living together for four years when they decided to have a baby. It was Jen who really wanted to; April was hesitant. April had felt more sexual intimacy with Jen than she had ever experienced before, and she worried about the impact a baby would have on their relationship. In the end, however, April gave in. She wanted to make Jen happy, and she wanted to seal their commitment.

At first, Jen tried to get pregnant through donor insemination. The process was emotionally and physically draining. Each month she would wait in suspense, only to later feel disappointed, frustrated, inadequate, and defeated. She knew it was irrational, but she felt like a failure as a woman, and the process left her depressed and withdrawn.

>

Eventually they agreed it was April's turn. She got pregnant on the first try. Jen was happy, but at the same time, she couldn't help feeling jealous. She began to resent all the attention April was getting from their friends. To cope, she started working longer hours at work and began volunteering for extra projects. Meanwhile, April felt uncomfortable, tired, needy, and miserable. She also felt anxious about childbirth and about being able to be a good parent. She worried her own unhappy upbringing would make her a bad mother. She needed Jen's support, but Jen was off in her own world.

Then Jason arrived. Instead of feeling the joys of motherhood, April felt not only exhausted, but also angry and hurt that Jen was so uninvolved. Moreover, she felt guilty about her feelings of resentment toward the little bundle of bodily functions that had taken over her life. Though she was the biological mother, she didn't really enjoy playing or cuddling with Jason the way Jen did. On the other hand, though Jen loved to play and snuggle, she couldn't remember to buy the groceries and couldn't keep a schedule; that was April's strongpoint. But when Jason cried, it was Jen, not April, who rushed to pick him up. Gradually, Jen began to see herself as the "real" mother. In her weaker moments, April, to her chagrin, thought she might be right.

One day, when doing her taxes, April found Jen's cell phone records, which showed multiple lengthy telephone calls to one number. April dialed it and recognized the name on the answering machine. It was Jen's coworker. Suddenly the pieces of a puzzle clicked into place: the late hours, the absences, the sexual indifference. An affair. She confronted Jen, who denied it all but also said nothing to reassure April of her love or commitment. In fact, what Jen said was, "You know I wouldn't do anything to take me away from the baby." April was devastated by this. Her worst fear was that Jen had just used her to have a baby, and this comment seemed to only confirm it. She felt tricked, exploited, and humiliated. In desperation, April reached out to her friend, Stephanie.

>

When Jason was only six months old, April moved in with Stephanie, who offered her the security and stability she desperately needed. Stephanie, however, had more romantic feelings for her. April talked herself into making love with Stephanie a few times, but the experience made her miss Jen. She told herself that it was more important to protect Jason and survive this crisis than it was for her to enjoy a sexual relationship. She settled into a peaceful and stable routine and prepared for the impending custody battle. Two years later, after a nightmare of legal suits and countersuits, each had 50 percent custody, and April owed $50,000 in legal fees. Her self-esteem was at rock bottom. She had lost Jen and gained a baby, a huge responsibility she was never sure she wanted in the first place. She was also in a relationship with a woman who was a good friend but not a lover.

The relationship with Stephanie lasted two years. Then April moved out, with enormous guilt but clear awareness that she could not offer Stephanie the kind of love she wanted. She berated herself for having moved in with her in the first place, but April also acknowledged that she had been too devastated and frightened to make rational decisions. Her biggest regret was that she and Jen hadn't been able to work through their conflicts. April said she could have forgiven the affair if she'd felt any hope that Jen could come back to her. Four years after she and Jen separated, April said she was still in love with her.

In her therapy sessions, April delved deeper into the reasons for her relationship collapse. She acknowledged that their prospects never looked very good. Neither one of them had very good motives for entering into parenthood. April hoped a child would secure her relationship with Jen, with whom she had been enjoying the best sexual intimacy in her life. Though she knew she was taking a risk, April hoped that becoming a parent with Jen would guarantee her lover would be at her side . . . at least for the next eighteen years. Jen's enthusiasm about motherhood, and the honor of being "chosen" as a coparent, skewed April's decision-making

>

abilities. Furthermore, it appeared that neither April nor Jen were fully cognizant of what to expect during fertility treatments, pregnancy, and early parenthood.

I didn't know Jen, so can only guess about what motivated her to begin an affair at the time she did. Like many coparents, she may have been very enthusiastic about the idea of a baby but shocked when the reality began to sink in. She may have been frightened by April's increasing dependence on her, both physically and emotionally. Most parents-to-be go through a phase of *Oh my God, what was I thinking? I can't handle this!* The lucky ones have family or friends they can turn to for reassurance—people who will remind them that everyone feels that way, but it will probably be okay. Jen wasn't so lucky. Her family totally disapproved of her relationship with April and their decision to have a child. Her friends didn't have children. No one who was close to Jen could talk to her about their own experience becoming parents, or help her develop more "team spirit" with April. Perhaps some encouragement to simply "hang in there" for the first year might have gotten both Jen and April through the very rough adjustment period and given them a chance to really develop a family. Perhaps.

Ironically, April and Jen's previously hot sexual relationship may have contributed to their problems. Sex for them had seemed spontaneous, and it was frequent. When the turnoffs of pregnancy cooled their ardor, they assumed the worst: Sexual intimacy is doomed. A more realistic understanding could have helped them nurture their sexual relationship more carefully. The self-esteem boost of feeling sexual and desirable could have encouraged them to turn toward each other for a deeper bond. They could have learned that intentionality trumps spontaneity when it comes to sustaining sexual satisfaction.

April and Jen's story is all too common among women seeking to become mothers. While I don't want to be discouraging about

>

parenthood, it needs to be pointed out that much unnecessary heartache is caused by the cultural expectation that women should seek joy and fulfillment through motherhood and through living for others instead of for themselves. This pressure is hard to escape and can induce guilt and shame among women who aren't that interested in becoming mothers. For some couples, a discrepancy in their desire for children can be a deal-breaker for the relationship. When two partners disagree about these basic values, painfully honest communication is needed to resolve the conflict.

Even those who are skilled at communication can lose those skills if they are going on four hours of sleep or if their hormones are off the chart because of fertility treatments or pregnancy. As a result, every couple needs to redouble their efforts toward honesty, understanding, listening and being supportive, and expressing fears during this time.

Even if such measures don't save a relationship, they can certainly help a couple in a dead-end relationship part amicably. In this case, a more amicable parting would have been far better for little Jason and far less strain on the lives of Jen and April. At the very least, it could have saved them a lot in legal fees.

One of the main reasons for the parental plunge in sexual intimacy is a lack of energy. Most couples don't anticipate the level of fatigue that a child brings. Keeping a baby or a toddler clean, clothed, and well fed is a daily, repetitive challenge, and most parents also have to figure out how to keep up a job, child care, and some semblance of order. It often seems there aren't enough hours in the day to manage all the new responsibilities, but there isn't an alternative—you have to keep the baby alive. When exhausted parents can squeeze in a few minutes for each other, they're usually so tired they'd rather sleep. Even if they could, many new parents would feel guilty about taking time alone when there is a baby in the house. Whenever you meet a person or a couple who's had a newborn within the last year, you can pretty much guarantee that they're suffering from sleep deprivation. And from there, it's a sort of chain reaction that, if not checked, can result in an explosion that pushes a couple apart—sometimes, unfortunately, for good. The chronic exhaustion (and with pregnancy and postpartum periods, a big fluctuation in hormones) leads to emotional volatility, depression, and feelings of isolation.

But even if they do manage to get a few good nights of sleep, few parents of small children would say they feel hungry for touch. A friend of mine once explained, "After having a baby hanging on me all day long, the last thing I want at night is another person hanging on me." She added, even with some anger, that her partner just felt like one more person wanting to use her body. What she really craved was to go to sleep peacefully, alone. She would need a great deal of rest, and warm-up time, before she would be able to enjoy touch of a different sort.

In a more general way, the type of identity change involved in mothering and caretaking is not conducive to sexual excitement. In fact, one of the major reasons women give for losing sexual interest in a partner is that the relationship has evolved into a parent–child dynamic. Many women say, "I feel like I'm taking care of two kids—the baby, and my partner." One partner may feel jealous of the other's attention toward the baby, and pout or complain to get equal time. The other may think, *Grow up! And help me more with the housework!* One partner may seem controlling and rigid, like a mother, while the other seems rebellious and irresponsible, like an adolescent. These roles are hard to shake off in the bedroom, especially when partners get polarized on different sides of the issue instead of working together as a team to overcome their shared obstacles.

In addition, parenthood brings more responsibility, less freedom, and a whole new set of conflicts about time, money, work, and priorities. These conflicts are additional opportunities for arguments between partners to develop. Having to make sacrifices (whether with work, spending, or time with friends and family) can lead to feelings of resentment, which are usually directed at the nearest adult—one's partner, who's probably feeling the same amount of stress.

And then there are conflicts about parenting styles. One parent is usually more strict, the other more lenient. One needs flexibility, the other needs routine. One is more focused on home and hearth, the other needs more outside contact. One is more playful and the other more task-oriented. Most parents really want what's best for their children, but may disagree about how to get there. These disagreements can easily degenerate into chronic conflict about who is right.

On top of all of this, lesbian couples also have their own special challenges. To start off with, we must show greater deliberation and motivation to become parents. We don't get pregnant the traditional way, or "accidentally." In fact, we usually have to go to a great deal of trouble, using awkward, emotionally complex, and often expensive methods like donor insemination, in-vitro fertilization, surrogacy, and adoption. In major cities with large queer populations, women can usually access gay-friendly doctors, clinics, and agencies to support their endeavors to have children. However, these resources are limited or nonexistent in less urban areas. Efforts to access these resources can drag on for years, wearing us down. And then there's discrimination. Lesbian couples have to hide their relationship in order to avoid prohibitions against gay adoptions. This dynamic is just asking for trouble. One person is designated as "mother" while the other recedes into invisibility. Meanwhile, the same demands for time and money and attention come pouring onto both partners, which can feel completely unfair to the one who's in the background.

For two female parents, conflicts over parenting styles may be even more intense. We're less likely to have gender-defined roles like "nurturing mother" and "breadwinning father," and we usually have more egalitarian expectations. We don't automatically assume "Mother knows best"—we're both mothers! It may be harder to turn over some areas of responsibility by simply saying, "That's not my role." Many women are surrounded all their lives with information and messages about mothering. Because of all that socialization, we may have equally strong viewpoints about what constitutes good parenting. It's hard to defer to other perspectives when they differ from ones we've learned so thoroughly.

Lesbian couples may also feel more competition over attention from their children. It's normal for babies and children to reach more for one parent than the other. In straight couples, the "preferred" parent is usually the mother, especially in infancy. Fathers may feel excluded or less important, but most of them expect this because of their gender-defined role. On the other hand, "nonpreferred" lesbian mothers may be more likely to feel hurt by this exclusion, and more likely to attribute it to something personal. Unfortunately, this can become a self-fulfilling prophecy, as one partner withdraws from the child to avoid feeling hurt and the other draws closer to compensate, resulting in further exclusion of the nonpreferred mother.

Sadly, we have few models of same-sex parents who have successfully negotiated these differences. Same-sex parenting is a relatively new phenomenon, exploding only in the past decade. Very few women who are old enough to be parents have grown up with examples of households with queer mothers. Furthermore, a majority of lesbian parents break up, so there are few successful, long-term models for us to emulate. Without a framework to manage the high-conflict, high-intensity emotions of parenthood, conditions are ripe for acting out in ways that bring relationships to a crashing halt.

For all couples in intense conflict, one of the most common forms of acting out involves having affairs. Feeling hurt, angry, and disappointed with each other, many new mothers turn to a new woman for comfort and relief. The sexual excitement of a new lover can be an antidote to feeling like the "chief cook and bottle-washer," or the sidelined, less-involved "other parent." The new lover doesn't have to negotiate diaper changes and bedtime routines. She can just be loving and supportive and replenish the well of good feelings. We may see how this is wrong, but most women who have experienced the stress of new parenting can understand how it happens. The stress can be too much to handle alone, and the partner relationship is often the biggest problem.

Unfortunately, an affair usually makes a bad situation worse. When it is discovered, which usually happens, there can be an explosion of panic and anger as both parents decide what to do next. The happily anticipated new family often dissolves into break-ups and custody fights.

It's tragic, given how much we've been fighting to change public opinion and perception of our community, but lesbian parents are notorious for getting involved in vicious custody battles. It's even more tragic because antigay legal biases capitalize on these individual, personal conflicts and are readily used to devalue or even destroy a child's emotional attachment to the "nonlegal" parent. These battles reinforce stereotypes of people in the queer community as "mentally unsound" and "unfit to be parents." For example, the statement "homosexual relationships are so unstable" is used to infer that we are inherently unable to sustain stable families. Instead of acknowledging that we don't get the same societal and family support for our relationships, many straight people assume we just aren't mature enough to parent properly. Those stereotypes not only hurt our public image; they also hurt our image of ourselves, which comes back to haunt us in weaker moments—moments of self-doubt that every person who's parenting or trying to get pregnant experiences.

An aftermath of many lesbian breakups is the rapid introduction of a new "stepmother." The old joke about lesbians bringing a U-Haul on the second date refers to the perception that women in love often move in together very quickly. The dark joke today is "Heather has twelve mommies." It's true that a new partner can ease the burden and help provide stability in a chaotic situation. But psychologists and family court judges worry about the psychological ramifications of rapidly shifting attachment figures. How does this affect a daughter's ability to form sexually intimate, long-term relationships when she grows up? What does a son learn about treating sexual partners with respect and dignity? How does this affect children's perceptions of their mother, whom they see bouncing in and out of intense, brief relationships? And how will the kids be able to grow up and leave her, when she can't seem to stand on her own? These are the troubling and unresolved questions that emerge in any divorce, questions we need to address in our queer community.

Linda and Ellen decided to adopt an infant daughter from China. After seven years together, they were eager to share their life and resources with a little girl, and knew that international adoptions from China were well managed and relatively problem-free. Their good friends had done this a few years before and gave them a great deal of information about how to handle the process. One vital piece of information was that only one of them could legally adopt, and she would have to sign a statement that she was "not a homosexual." Neither Linda nor Ellen liked the idea of having to be deceptive, but they agreed that it was worth it, under the circumstances. After all, no adoption agency would agree to help them adopt as a same-sex couple. Linda looked more heterosexual and family-oriented on paper. She had been married before and she still had a good relationship with her ex-husband and their respective families. Ellen agreed that it would be easier for Linda to "pass" as a heterosexual woman, so she became the "designated mother." It was hard for Ellen at first to accept her invisibility in the process, but it was also clear that it was necessary to make this happen.

>

Before a social worker came to do a home study, Ellen removed some of her items from the bedside table and then disappeared. The social worker spent two hours with Linda, walking through the home to see where the baby's room would be and how the house was organized. Linda presented herself as a divorced woman who had developed a stable life on her own. Almost a year after the home study, Linda received a picture of a little girl who was being referred to her. She and Ellen wept together over the picture and began planning their trip to China. They left four months later.

On the trip to China, Ellen presented herself as a "family friend" who was there to help Linda manage traveling with a baby. Throughout all the different steps in the Chinese adoption process, Ellen stayed in the background and was careful not to be affectionate with Linda or the baby. She was afraid someone would suspect them of being lesbian and would deny the adoption at the last minute. They kept a careful distance from each other. Ellen watched from across the room, feeling excluded and anxious, while Linda officially became their baby's mother.

During their time in China, Linda and Ellen treated themselves to a five-star hotel. "Usually, staying somewhere like that would be a vacation for us," Ellen said. "We'd feel more relaxed and pampered than we would at home, and we'd probably make love more often. Instead, we both felt so tense, and we didn't even feel like we were a couple any more. I started thinking I really *was* just a family friend who came along to help out," Ellen said. "One night, before we got the baby, we joked about trying to have sex, as if it were the craziest idea imaginable. It would have been like swimming against the current, definitely not the right mood." They were both obsessed with thoughts about the baby and couldn't imagine switching into a more erotic mood.

For several months after they came back from China with their little girl, Linda and Ellen weren't able to create the mood for sexual intimacy.

>

Fortunately, they were able to talk honestly about their feelings. Both of them were more exhausted than they had expected. They were thrilled with their daughter but tired of the relentless focus on her. Ellen shared with Linda that she had felt peripheral to the adoption process and feared that might continue in their family life. Linda said she had felt alone in the responsibility to make the process go smoothly. Both of them were able to understand each other's perspective and to validate that each had different challenges to face. Talking this honestly helped them reestablish an emotional connection that had been lost under the ordeals of adoption.

After getting more connected emotionally, Linda and Ellen realized that they were missing their sexual connection as well. The problem was how to make enough time and space. They reached out to friends who also had children. These friends understood completely and offered to trade babysitting nights so they could go out at least twice a month. It was an arrangement that worked well for all of them. After a few months of trying this arrangement, Linda and Ellen actually left their little girl with these friends overnight. They went to a cabin for a wonderful time with each other. Their daughter giggled and cooed with their friends' children.

Seeing their daughter having fun with other children made Linda and Ellen aware of something they hadn't fully recognized. Seeing their little girl in an orphanage in China had made them both feel more protective of her, and very anxious to assure her that she would never again be abandoned. At some level, both had feared that she would feel abandoned if they left her with friends overnight. But seeing her have a good time with others made them realize they were raising a secure daughter who actually benefited from relating to other people, not just them. Most of all, they felt how their own intimate reconnection made them happier with each other and with their little family.

IT TAKES A great deal of planning and intention for lesbian couples to become mothers—and it takes even more intentionality for them to remain lovers over the long haul. A big part of this practice of intentionality is being very explicit about needing time with just each other. This can involve asking family or friends to stay with the children so they can get away, as well as being open about a need for private time with each other. Lesbian couples need to take extra responsibility for this, especially because we are less likely to be reminded of the importance of quality time alone with each other. Lesbian parents are less likely than straight parents to hear "Be sure to save time for each other," because our sexuality and our relationships are not valued as much by society. It's possible that lesbian mothers receive less support from their own mothers or other relatives, simply because they are more likely to be estranged from the family of origin.

Fortunately, lesbian friends are famous for stepping in to help when needed, so this may compensate for some lack of family support. Some queer parents have developed very creative ways to help each other with child care. In one group of four mothers, each mother alternates keeping all of the children one Saturday night so the others can have a night out. In other words, each mother gets three free Saturday nights per month. Other groups take vacations together so that they can take turns watching the children while each parent, or couple, gets a few hours alone. Usually, help arrives in more informal ways, as when a friend simply offers to help out. It's important to let your friends know that you'd appreciate some help, and to offer ways to compensate them so it's worth their while.

As you may already know because of Hillary Rodham Clinton's book, there is a Nigerian proverb that goes "It takes a village to raise a child." It takes a village for parents to maintain their sexual intimacy. One of the most essential ingredients to protecting your sexual bond with your partner is to have a good support system, a.k.a. "babysitters." For many parents, the only way to keep having sex after parenthood is to leave town. Locks on bedroom doors are important, but for some, a geographic boundary is needed. A friend of mine once said, laughing but serious, that she seemed to need at least "two days and sixty miles of separation" before she could get herself in the mood. She has lots of company. Many women need to be physically out of reach of the children before they can reach for a sexual partner. When they find the space to do that, they remember the wonderful bonding that sex can offer and why it's worth the effort.

Many lesbian couples may be uncomfortable with being that open with their friends and family—and with each other—about rather blatantly setting up a sexual scenario for themselves. Several factors may interfere. To some, it may even feel like inviting the village to watch an illicit activity. We don't usually have a whole network of people sending us off on a honeymoon, which could be an equivalent heterosexual ritual. Also, there's more social support for women mothering than for going off together for a sexual rendezvous. We've internalized that reinforcement and find it far too easy to get consumed in parenting and ignore intimacy needs. We've also internalized tremendous responsibility for children and may feel guilty about turning them over to someone else just so we can have some personal pleasures. There are many logical arguments against taking the space and time just for each other, but it's essential in order to create conditions for sexual intimacy.

If protecting your sexual intimacy with your partner drops to the bottom of your priority list, you are not only cheating yourselves. You are also cheating your children. Most of us want our children to grow up and eventually have a relationship that's both emotionally and sexually fulfilling. How are we going to help them achieve that if we don't give them a model to work with? If we instead demonstrate an obsessive focus on parenting, a disinterest in our partner, and a life of personal sacrifice, is it reasonable to expect that our children won't follow in our unfulfilled footsteps?

Seeing two adults who are both committed and romantic with each other is a wonderful gift for our children, and for ourselves. It's extremely unfortunate that it is such a rarely given gift. In our preoccupation with being good parents, we forget that our children learn most from observing us. It's good for them to know that adults have something special and private that they too can grow into someday. They can see the tender attention, and the warm afterglow, and know that something magical is happening. It's accessible magic. Doing something like reading this book, talking with your partner about your intimate life, making time just for each other—these are ways to bring magic into your relationship, and thereby into your family. Believe me, your children will appreciate it!

Your Turn

① Think about how your own early family life affected your expectations about sexuality in the context of a family. How did your parents treat each other when you were a child? Were you aware of some special, positive energy between them? Were there overt messages about your parents' sexuality? What kind of boundaries do you remember your parents setting with you? Reflecting on these questions can help you discover if you really, deep down, believe that it's okay for parents to sometimes ignore their children and just focus on each other.

② If you're thinking about forming a family, talk with your partner about your own family values. Do you think sexual intimacy is important after parenthood? Should your children know about it? How will you talk with them about sex, and about lesbian sex? It's important for the two of you to understand each others values and expectations and to agree on how you'll discuss these issues with your children. They will need to hear most from you about this topic, to counteract the antigay rhetoric they are sure to hear from the outside world.

③ If you and your partner are already parents, what kind of dynamics have you noticed between the two of you? Do you feel treated like a parent or a child? Does your partner? When are the times that you both feel like you're really working as a team, and when are you on opposing sides? Can you be on the same team when it comes to creating sexual intimacy for each other?

④ What are some of the ways you and your partner talk yourselves out of taking some private time with each other, like going on a date? Talk to her about this. Do some of these feel like excuses, or ways to avoid being intimate? Do you have some fears about what will happen to your child if you leave her with someone else briefly? Talk to each other about how rational those fears are.

⑤ Do either of you feel excluded by the other parent? Jealous of her attention to the child? Left out of a happy twosome or treated as unimportant and peripheral? What would help you feel more involved and appreciated?

⑥ Talk with each other, and with other gay parents, about how to affirm sexuality at home and how to use good boundaries and judgment to protect your children from antigay comments or bullying at school.

⑦ Check out resources that support queer parents, like the Mega Family Project, or gay-affirmative churches and synagogues. Some of these may offer workshops or literature on supporting sexuality between same-sex parents while giving children age-appropriate information.

secrets to longlasting intimacy

9

Communication for Lovers

IN THE BEGINNING of a relationship, the words seem to come so easily. That's probably because they're usually all so positive. When new lovers say, "We made love and talked all night," you can guess what the talk was like: "You're the best." "I've never felt like this before." "I can't wait to be with you again." Those sweet words spring out effortlessly, fueled by romance and falling-in-love chemicals. You love to say these things, and to hear them, and there's no problem communicating. Not yet.

The difficulty in talking sets in later, when the honeymoon is over and everything isn't 100 percent positive. And of *course* it isn't 100 percent positive. Perfect compatibility is rare—and that's a good thing. It's the rough edges that can make you grow, both as a person and as a couple, because you have to take risks and step outside your comfort zone if you want more intimacy.

No matter who you are, or what your circumstances, there's one thing you're going to have to do if you want to enrich your intimacy with your partner: You're going to have to communicate with her about sex. Skillfully. And not just once. You'll need to talk often, and freely, about your sexual feelings. You'll also need to listen, attentively and nonjudgmentally, while she talks about hers.

In addition to the sharing of valuable information, there's another important benefit of this kind of communication. The very act of talking about sexual wants and worries can deepen your trust and sense of intimacy with each other. There's a great emotional connection that happens when you can be vulnerable with each other, expressing secret fears and keeping an open heart, and mind. And it all starts with words.

Some corporations use "ropes courses" as a way to build teamwork. This is where you have to step off a ledge and trust your teammates to catch you before you hit the ground. The reason ropes courses work is because first you're afraid, then you're relieved, then you feel a surge of trust. You know you can trust your teammates because they caught you, they didn't let you hit the ground. If there's no fear, then there's also no relief, no deepening of trust. It's the element of risk that makes the trust happen.

Sex is a lot like the ropes courses. You announce your intentions, take off your clothes, and trust your partner to catch you in an intimate embrace. When you show her your nude body, you face the fears most of us have about body image: *Am I too fat? Too flat? Too wrinkled? Too much? Too little?* You hope that she will respond to you with sexual desire, and that she won't leave you feeling exposed and foolish. After you start making love, you might also need to trust her to "read" you accurately and not leave you hanging halfway between arousal and orgasm. And at some point, you'll need to risk telling her about what feels good and what doesn't. Another risk, another opportunity to deepen your trust.

At the time we first talked, Jennifer hadn't had sex with her partner in four years. She had been very conflicted about sex with Hilary, whom she loved and was very attracted to, but who was too fast and aggressive in bed for her taste. She attempted to resolve the conflict by withdrawing sexually. Hilary was hurt and angry, and after a year of repeatedly initiating and getting rejected, she withdrew also.

When Jennifer talked about her sexual experiences with Hilary, a clear internal conflict became apparent. Hilary was a "rapid responder." She loved fast, firm stimulation, and that's how she touched Jennifer. But Jennifer wasn't built the same way and was much slower to get aroused and reach orgasm. She usually felt overstimulated by Hilary's approach. Her clitoris was telling her, *This feels uncomfortable,* but her heart was saying, *I don't want to hurt her feelings,* and based on past experiences with Hilary's temper, her mind was saying, *I don't want to make her mad.* "Maybe it's me," she wondered aloud. "Maybe I don't respond the way I should."

Jennifer's "maybe it's me" conclusion is one many women make. It's part of our tendency to adapt to others' standards. *If this doesn't feel good, there must be something wrong with my feeling receptors.* It would be exactly like thinking *If you like asparagus and I don't, that there must be something wrong with my taste buds.* Not true! We just have different taste buds. We're two different people! We're different in bed too, and that's a good thing.

When Jennifer and Hilary finally talked honestly, both were surprised by some of what they discovered. Hilary didn't mind slowing down at all. She said she had thought she wasn't doing enough to get Jennifer turned on, so that was why she tried too hard. It was a relief to her to know that she didn't have to work so hard. She could relax more while making love to Jennifer, go much slower, and try to follow Jennifer's lead instead of forging ahead. Meanwhile, Jennifer felt tremendously relieved that Hilary didn't get angry or act devastated. She felt validated when Hilary said she knew everyone has different thresholds for stimulation. Most of all,

>

Jennifer felt a surge of self-respect when she was able to tell Hilary what she wanted differently. They decided to make a fresh start on their sexual relationship, as if they were dating for the first time and getting to know what each other liked. A phone call from Jennifer several months later let me know their new relationship was going well.

Rules, Guidelines, and Techniques

Because communicating about sex can make you feel vulnerable, it's important to go over some rules and guidelines. Following them will not only protect you both from hurt feelings, but it will teach you how to talk to each other honestly about tough subjects with a deep sense of respect.

RULES

Let's start with three ground rules that must never be broken. These are the rules about what *not* to do, ever, when communicating about sex. If you think they're a little overzealous, just spend five minutes thinking about how you would feel if your partner broke one with you.

① Never insult or ridicule your partner's sexual behavior, mannerisms, appearance, or particular quirks. Those comments can sting very deeply, and they're not forgotten.

② Never compare your partner to previous lovers. This is extremely rude and it will backfire on you. She'll probably wonder what you might say about her some day.

③ Never complain about your sex life to mutual friends. We all have the right to decide how much our good friends know about our private sexual lives, and a partner doesn't have the right to decide that for you. Of course, you need to talk with close friends— just pick one who's close to you but not close to your partner.

GUIDELINES

There are also some important guidelines to follow if you want to create an atmosphere that feels safe for vulnerability and honesty with each other.

① Be gentle. Sex is a sensitive subject for many women. So many of us harbor feelings of inadequacy or insecurity, wanting to please our partners but being afraid we're not "performing" well enough. An offhand comment can strike a nerve that you didn't even know about, especially because we're likely to keep those feelings hidden. Saying "I want to understand more about what oral sex is like for you," is more gentle than "Tell me why you seem so uninterested in oral sex." Similarly, you might feel better hearing "I'd like to hold you in bed" than "When are you coming to bed?" "What helps you feel more relaxed?" probably works better than "You seem really uptight." As always, the Golden Rule helps—if you need to tell her something difficult, think of how you'd like her to tell you the same thing. Chances are you'd prefer a soft touch to harsh bluntness.

② Be positive. When it comes to communication, being positive means using language that avoids negatives such as "don't," "not," "isn't," "doesn't." It never helps to criticize or complain, so focus on building on what works instead of tearing down what doesn't work. It's also important to be complimentary when you get what you like; this reinforces what you've achieved together. The following are some examples of positive statements:

- "When I'm close to orgasm, it feels extra good if you . . ."
- "I like it when you touch me here . . ."
- "I really enjoy how you . . ."
- "It feels great when . . ."
- "I love being able to take a little more time to . . ."
- "It's easiest for me to have an orgasm when you . . ."
- "I feel wonderful when you let me . . ."

Sometimes it takes some forethought and practice to reframe criticisms into positive outcomes, but it's work that's good for both partners. It may involve focusing on positive experiences you've had together in the past and asking for more of those. Or you may highlight something that your partner does that you really enjoy, and tell her why you like that so much. Or you can talk about how you're either similar or a little different in some of the things you enjoy most.

The key is to tie any requests to a positive experience. That way you'll create a positive association with your request, and she'll have a concrete example of what you want. You won't have to feel guilty about hurting her feelings, or worry that she'll retaliate by putting you down later. Instead, you can feel good that you're helping both of you have even more enjoyable sexual experiences together. Focusing on what's positive in your sexual relationship is a boost to self esteem for both of you and will make it easier the next time you want to talk about something sexual.

③ Be outside the bedroom. After all, you don't want your bedroom to feel like a clinical learning laboratory! That might seem obvious to some, but it doesn't dawn of many of us to make sure the bedroom doesn't become the classroom. For many women—but not all—it's hard to deintellectualize sex in the same place that they've intellectualized it. If this means you, it can help to find a neutral place and time to talk about sex, when you're alone together and in no hurry. Long drives in the country are great places to talk about sexual specifics. Not everyone can attend an intimacy workshop, but these are also a healthy space for couples to communicate about their sex together.

④ Be honest. The bottom line is that if you want something sexually, you need to let your partner know. If she's doing something that's a turn-off, you need to let her know that too. There's just no way to keep your sexual relationship lively and satisfying if you don't talk honestly with each other.

Speaking up honestly about sexual issues is difficult for many women. We tend to worry about hurting each other's feelings and are too quick to set our own aside. Our capacity for empathy is wonderful, but sometimes it's too much of a good thing. If I'm too busy trying to feel your feelings, I may discount mine. Then I don't get what I need, and you don't either, because you're not getting a whole person—you're getting the fragments that I think you can handle.

That's fundamentally disrespectful to both of us. If I really think you can't handle hearing that I want something different in bed, I'm not giving you much credit. Being honest with you means that I respect you as a responsible and caring adult who doesn't get her feelings crushed just because I might like something different.

We often resist speaking up not only because we're afraid of hurt feelings, but also because we think our needs and desires should be automatically known by our lovers. I think that deep inside, we still wish things were the same as when we were babies, when we could expect others to know what we need and to provide it, without having to ask. It can make us feel indignant when they don't, and we find ourselves thinking, *Why am I having to ask? If she loved me, she would already know. If I have to ask for it, it doesn't count!* You get the picture.

But when babies get bigger and become toddlers, they learn to speak and express their wants and needs, and they're elated about it—even a little power-hungry: "You can't make me!" And "I can do it myself!" They find that the one thing better than having a parent to anticipate your every need is having your own voice, so you can express your needs yourself.

As adults, there's joy that comes from finding your sexual voice, being able to tell your partner what you want, and learning that she respects your wishes. That joy makes it worth the trouble of facing your anxiety about being honest.

Existential psychologists talk a lot about "authenticity." Authenticity is the sense of saying what we really feel and mean, speaking the truth about our own experiences. It's the opposite of adapting what I say to fit someone else's needs. Sometimes it's called "being yourself," and it's a wonderful feeling. We feel grounded, centered, transparent, and powerful, because energy is flowing straight from our hearts into our words and actions. And how wonderful it is to feel that while making love. That's what honesty—being authentic—can do for you.

⑤ Be selfish/assertive. When women start being honest, they may encounter another internal obstacle, an inner voice that tells them, *Don't be selfish!*

When we were growing up and learning about sex, what most of us learned was that sex is something men really want. We learned to think about what pleases them, not ourselves. In fact, we learned that so well that often we don't even know what *we* want. Even if we do know, the act of putting focus on ourselves seems to complete contradict our cultural training. To many, it seems like the antithesis of being a good lover.

But sexual selfishness contains a paradox. If my partner knows that I indulge in a healthy amount of sexual selfishness, she doesn't ever have to wonder whether or not I'm satisfied with our lovemaking, because if I'm not, she knows that I'm "selfish" enough to make it a priority, and that I will make it known to her (in a constructive, supportive, loving way, of course). That kind of knowledge actually is a turn-on! My lover can be confident that we both know what turns me on, and that confidence in being able to please me will then turn her on. She will feel like a great lover.

⑥ Be specific. In my workshops, I have each participant write down a list of specific things her partner does that help her feel aroused.

Couples then go off in a corner and read their responses to each other—not "talk about" their responses, but read them to each other. Something about having to simply read what they've already written down seems to keep them honest. If asked to "talk about this with your partner," most women won't get specific enough. It's not uncommon for me to hear afterward, "I'm glad you made us write this down first, because I could never have told her that. It just seems too . . . bold!"

Most women, even if they've been with their partners for a long time, are surprised at what they hear. There are usually comments like, "I didn't know you liked that!" and "I always wondered why we started doing that . . . " or even "What a relief! That always bothered me too!"

Some women are stunned when they realize how hard it is to talk about sex so specifically. I'm not. When we were young, we weren't supposed to be having sex at all, so how should we know how to talk about it? Once we got old enough for sex, we were still not supposed to talk about it—we were supposed to be carried away by passion, and everything was supposed to just happen naturally. We also might have picked up along the way that talking about sex might make our partners think we knew too much about it, or reveal that we didn't know enough about it. And on top of the "slutty" or "frigid" labels we wanted to avoid, our society and culture also has often portrayed women who talk about sex as too demanding, aggressive, domineering, and even threatening. So many of us learned not to talk.

Even if we can eschew those labels, sometimes we are afraid that talking about sex makes it too clinical, and therefore has a dampening effect on passion. Au contraire. In my intimacy work-shops, after couples spend some time reading their "turn-on" lists to each other, they usually come back to the group discussion look-ing a little mischievous. Usually at least one woman will say she got turned on writing and telling her partner what she likes sexually. Then several others will grin and nod. What's a turn-off is the psy-chological self-analysis that too many women get into instead of just saying what they like. Sometimes I've heard women give lengthy explanations of how they probably have control issues stemming from childhood insecurities, when what they really mean is that they want to be touched differently. I want to encourage them, and you, to be gentle and positive, and just ask for what you want. There's an excellent chance you'll both get a charge out of that.

Dacia and Alice had been partners for thirteen years and had sex once or twice a month. They were pleased with their quantity but disappointed in the quality of their sexual experiences, because they often ended in some disagreement. When they came for a consultation, both spoke very freely. It was obvious that verbal expression wasn't the problem—it was the listening.

Dacia's partner loved to penetrate her vaginally, but Dacia didn't like that very much. At best, it gave her a pleasant, full feeling; at worst, it was irritating. She was afraid her partner would feel embarrassed, or offended, if she told her she didn't like vaginal penetration and would have preferred much more clitoral stimulation. For a long time, Dacia told herself that she shouldn't be selfish and deprive her partner of something she enjoyed doing so much. She also began to question her own sexual

>

responses and wondered if "normal" women liked vaginal penetration more than she did

After a few years, Dacia gathered her courage to tell Alice that she really didn't like vaginal penetration. As she had feared, Alice was offended. Instead of listening carefully, asking Dacia to tell her more about how penetration felt to her, Alice reacted with judgment. She told Dacia that her previous partners had loved vaginal penetration, and she thought the problem was that Dacia couldn't relax enough. To Alice, being able to penetrate her partner was the epitome of intimacy. She said nothing else gave her quite the same feeling of complete connection, and she loved it. Furthermore, she thought it was "abnormal" that Dacia did not. Alice had suggested the consultation in hopes that I could help Dacia learn to relax more during sex so she could enjoy vaginal penetration.

After listening to both women talk about their frustration around this repetitive issue, I told them that many women don't care for penetration, and most women feel more pleasure from clitoral stimulation. This was a shock to Alice. None of her previous partners had discussed this issue with her, so she'd assumed everyone liked it as much as she did. She also hadn't realized how judgmental she sounded. Much to her credit, Alice was able to back off and take in some new information. Dacia was relieved and eager to work out a compromise. She told Alice she'd enjoy vaginal penetration but only after she'd had an orgasm, because that was when it felt best. That way both could get more of what they wanted. They both left feeling better, and they called six months later to say "Thanks! We're doing great!"

TECHNIQUES

① Use "I-statements." If you want to be heard, start with talking about yourself. Contrast the following and imagine how you'd respond to each.

- "I miss the good feelings I used to have when we made love."
- "You don't make love with me enough."
- "I wish we could have some romantic time together this weekend."
- "You stay too busy on the weekend."
- "I really enjoy your touch when you keep a slow and steady rhythm with me."
- "You touch me too fast."

These aren't subtle differences. One statement is talking about myself and what I feel or want, and the other sounds like I'm blaming or criticizing you.

A general hint is to be careful about any sentence that starts with the word "you." It's a word that puts most people on alert: What's coming next? A compliment? Criticism? Complaint? Advice? A "you-statement" sounds like an effort to blame or "fix" your partner, and it won't be appreciated. In fact, it's a real conversation-stopper.

An "I-statement" is a sincere effort to let your partner understand you better. Notice also how the I-statements above include the positive desired outcome: making love, having romantic time together, having a slow steady rhythm.

② Engage in active listening. It's not always easy to listen. Hearing things we don't want to hear makes most of us anxious.

One way to handle that anxiety is to tune out anything that seems threatening. I remember one client who told me, "I kept telling my new partner I needed her to slow down in bed, but she didn't seem to hear me. She liked to be touched fast and had orgasms really quickly, but I need more time to get there, so I kept hinting, then I told her explicitly to go slower . . . but she wasn't changing. So finally I had to talk to her when we weren't in bed and spell it out. She said she'd been so nervous about trying to please me, and she thought I liked what she did. She finally heard me, and sex got much better, but it still bothered me that she wasn't paying attention earlier. I wondered what else she wasn't paying attention to."

Another very common way of handling threatening feedback is to formulate a comeback while the other person is still talking. Planning a defense, counterattacking, and thinking about how to appease or reassure the other person are all ways to try to decrease anxiety. Of course, all of these involve not really paying attention, so of course they don't help us understand the other person's feelings or point of view. This is the kind of *not* listening that leaves people feeling misunderstood, frustrated, and alienated from each other.

It's easy to affirm the importance of honesty in intimate relationships, but STIs (sexually transmitted infections) can really test your values. Will you be honest when it may mean losing someone you really want? Will you be able to be nonjudgmental? Can you stay lovingly, sexually engaged with a woman when one of you has an STI that could affect the spontaneity of your lovemaking?

Obviously, self-disclosure is the key—very early self-disclosure, and definitely before putting anyone at risk. In fact, it's becoming more common for new couples to get tested before starting any sexual contact; some even go to get tested at the same time. Then they actually show

>

each other their test results, which is the most convincing, reassuring, and responsible route. I recommend doing this no matter whether you've already tested positive or negative in the past for STIs. It's courteous and responsible, and it sets up an excellent foundation of trust and reliability, which are two outstanding qualities to have in any new relationship. If you feel awkward suggesting this, you could always just get tested on your own, offer the results, and wait for her reaction. Usually, she too will get the hint and do the same. If she doesn't respond in kind, or if she otherwise avoids the issue, that's a big red flag, and you have to ask yourself how much you can trust her in an ongoing relationship.

Women who get tested before starting a new relationship are smart. After all, even if you were negative a while ago and haven't had sex since, some STIs take a significant amount of time to show up on tests. But it can be scary to get tested, especially when you're uncertain about what the results might be: *What if I test positive for something? How could I tell her?* Herpes in particular is becoming more common, and it's a hard diagnosis to accept because there is not yet a cure, and because the taboo associated with it is out of proportion with the health risks. Many who find out they have herpes end up overwhelmed and confused by conflicting or vague information about testing accuracy, health risks, transmission risks, and other factual information.

For some fortunate women, the new sexual partner is gracious enough to accept news of an STI with respect and gratitude, and the whole experience becomes an excellent proving ground for communication, trust, and respect. Others may lose out on a new relationship because of it. That can be a blow. I've heard some women say, "I'll never have sex again because of this." Fortunately, later I've heard the same women say, "I met someone and we figured out how to manage the herpes, and sex is great!" Sure, it's risky to tell the truth, but it's disastrous not to. It's about safety and respect, and both of those are essential foundations to a relationship.

>

It may seem as though there's never a good time to say, "I've tested positive for herpes." But if you think that's hard, imagine how hard it would be to say, after several months of dating, "By the way, I noticed a rash, so I went to the doctor, and it turns out I have herpes. Chances are, you do too." The damage that can do to a long-term relationship is much harder to deal with than temporary pain of losing a fledgling romance.

Much has been said about the difficulty of talking about STIs when starting a new relationship. But not much has been said about the difficulty of *continuing* to talk about them in an established relationship, or about dealing with the discovery of an STI while already in a relationship. Even if you've already had the STI talk, it will come up again; for example, herpes outbreaks can happen any time and can certainly change your plans for a hot weekend together. If it's your herpes, you'll need to let your partner know that you're having symptoms of an impending outbreak, and that you regret how this is interfering with plans you made together. If she's the one telling you about an outbreak, you'll need to be as gentle and positive as possible, and let her know you're still glad to be her partner and look forward to making love however/whenever you can.

The biggest challenge is when you have to let an established partner know you've just discovered an STI you didn't know you had. If you're supposedly in a monogamous relationship and your partner does not have an STI, you can see the problem. How did you get it? Obviously, if this was acquired through infidelity, you may have to confess. It isn't fair to withhold that kind of information when it impacts your partner too. However, there are some STIs that take a long time to show up, so it is possible that you (or she) unknowingly brought it into your relationship. Regardless of how one of you acquired an STI, both of you need to be tested. Furthermore, you may need to be retested if it's possible you've been infected but it hasn't shown up yet. You can see why brutal honesty is the simplest route to take.

>

Open communication about sex and STIs isn't limited to your sexual partner. In order to get the healthcare women need and deserve, they need to be open and honest with their doctors. Unfortunately, many doctors are not well informed about lesbian sexual practices and therefore may give irrelevant advice, if any at all.[A] But the doctors are not the only culprits. Many studies suggest that lesbians are less likely to get routine medical examinations, and that they are less likely to discuss their sex lives with their doctors.[B] These avoidant patterns place us at higher risk for asymptomatic or seemingly minor health problems that can cause serious damage if left untreated. To protect all of us from the consequences of STIs, we must be able to talk freely with our doctors and other healthcare providers about our sex lives. This means identifying doctors who are gay-affirmative and pushing ourselves to be as open as possible about our sexual relationships with women. Several organizations publish guides to gay-friendly doctors. Though they have headquarters in specific cities, they often have information for people living in other regions.

- The Mautner Project (Washington, D.C.)
  www.mautnerproject.org

- The Lesbian Health Project (University of California, San Francisco)
  www.lesbianhealthinfo.org

- Gay and Lesbian Medical Association (San Francisco)
  www.glma.org

- The Atlanta Lesbian Health Initiative
  www.thehealthinitiative.org

Yet another way we might deal with the anxiety of hearing difficult things is to attack the speaker with reassurance. When your partner expresses a desire for something different from you, it's easy to jump to, "Of course, whatever you want is fine with me, don't worry about that." That may sound reassuring, but it's a little condescending, and it shortchanges the process. It doesn't let her fully express how she feels about the issue; it doesn't make you have to listen to something that might make you uncomfortable. Putting a reassuring bandage on her discomfort precludes the opportunity for a deeper dialogue that actually helps both of you understand each other better. A little reassurance can help, but it should come later, after you've given the process a chance to work.

Besides learning to tell your partner what you like and need to enjoy sex the most, it's equally important to pay attention to what she tells you. The best way to do this is to practice a type of listening that involves paraphrasing and reflecting the other person's feelings. It's a powerful, effective method that is very healing and helpful. For simplicity, I'm calling it "active listening" here. It's simple, but not easy, and it's extremely worth the effort. Why? Because it builds empathy, and empathy works magic in relationships.

By engaging in active listening, you can almost guarantee that you'll be paying attention, and that the person you're listening to will know you're paying attention. The goal is first to understand, then to be understood, and it follows a specific format. There's a Talker and a Listener. When the Talker speaks, the other listens attentively, especially to any emotions that are being expressed. After the Talker says a few sentences, she gives the Listener a chance to respond. The Listener paraphrases what she heard the Talker say— again, with special emphasis on any emotions that were expressed. The Listener says *only* what the Talker said—she doesn't insert her own opinions, feelings, or editorial comments. Her goal is to really understand how the Talker feels, and to make sure the Talker knows that she understands. The Listener ends her paraphrase with a request for confirmation that she understood correctly; something like, "Is that right?" works well.

Both the Listener and the Talker should place an emphasis on feelings. Why? Because sharing feelings is the core of intimate relating. If I tell you my mother died, and you change the subject or tell me your mother died too, I'm not going to feel closer to you. But if you hear my sadness, I'll feel understood and comforted, and will probably want to tell you more. The context and details aren't nearly as important as the emotions involved. So when you listen, listen for feelings, and when you talk, try to talk about your feelings. You'll make more progress toward intimate connection.

Active listening is very simple—and very hard to do, because difficult conversations usually involve negative feelings, and it's hard to listen to those without jumping to defense or reassurance. It takes effort to pay attention, self-discipline to hold back your immediate reactions, and faith that this process will work. And it will. It's amazing how quickly people can get off a stuck position when they feel understood and respected. But you have to give them a chance, and that means you have to do the work to understand. Here's an example of using active listening.

TALKER: I want to talk to you about something, but I'm afraid you'll get upset.

LISTENER: So you want us to talk, but you're nervous about my reaction. Is that right?

TALKER: Yes, I don't mean to sound critical. Sometimes I'll think we're going to make love, and then you'll answer the telephone. That makes me feel like the phone call is more important than me, which hurts my feelings and makes me mad too.

LISTENER: Okay. My answering the phone when we're going to make love hurts your feelings, and makes you mad, because it seems like the phone call is more important than you. Is that right?

TALKER: Yeah. It could be anyone on the phone, and I'm right here, and you seem more worried about ignoring them than ignoring me. That's why it bothers me so much.

LISTENER: It really bothers you a lot, because it seems like you're not as important to me as whoever happens to be on the phone. Did I get that right?

TALKER: Yes! Wouldn't that bother you?

You may be reading this dialogue thinking, *Why do you need to keep repeating what she just said? Doesn't that feel stupid after awhile?* But think about your usual reaction when someone expresses negative feelings toward you. You probably start planning a defense, or a counterattack, or reassurance, just to escape the situation. At some level, that's what your partner expects when she talks about difficult subjects, so the minute you show her your intention to really listen and understand her point of view, she'll probably be shocked. She'll realize that you do care and do want things to be better for both of you, and that will soften any hard feelings she's holding toward you.

The whole point of paraphrasing what your partner is saying is that it builds empathy between you. It's a way of being fully present with another person. In other words, instead of going off in your head to prepare your response, you choose to stay tuned in and pay attention to *her*. You're letting her know that her feelings are important to you, and that you care enough to really listen even when she's saying things that are hard for you to hear. You aren't taking a leave of absence. You're present, and your undivided attention is a wonderful gift that's going to come back to you, many times over.

Anne was a forty-two-year-old woman with a teenager's glee about her weekend date. After two years of mourning the end of her long-term relationship, she had met someone she really liked. They had several coffees and lunches, moved on to dinners, and then had the talk about Where This Is Going. Apparently, it was going the same place for both of them: the bedroom.

On their next date, Val gave Anne a copy of her recent testing report, showing her as negative for any STIs. Anne got the hint and scheduled an appointment for her own testing at the local women's health clinic. Anne laughed to herself about how grown-up and responsible she was being, especially given that she hadn't slept with anyone since her breakup, which had taken place more than a year ago. She fully expected a clean bill of health, and looked forward to her next date with Val.

A few days later, Anne called me in shock. She had tested positive for genital herpes. Now she remembered that a very few times in her last long-term relationship, she had experienced a slight burning and stinging sensation in her genitals but had assumed it was just because she wasn't used to being sexually active. Ironically Anne had ended her last relationship because she longed for more sexual enjoyment. Her last partner had given Anne very little sexually. What she did give her was herpes. Anne was understandably very upset. She had been so excited about sharing sexual intimacy with Val, who seemed so open and caring and equally interested in sex. "This was supposed to be my time," she cried.

>

Anne needed some time to deal with her feelings about having herpes. She felt angry at her ex-partner and sad about losing her hopes for unfettered sexuality. She was also embarrassed to tell Val and afraid that this might be a deal-breaker for their romance. We talked at length about how she could cope with Val's response. It could be very disappointing, we agreed, but it also could be revealing. Val's response to this information would tell Anne a lot about what a long-term relationship could be like with her. For example, Val might be very understanding while also showing that she respected herself enough to take appropriate precautions in a gentle and diplomatic way. Or she might back away abruptly. Or she might deny that it bothered her, but never call again. Different options, all yielding great information about what it would be like to partner with Val. So Anne gathered her courage up and went to talk about her herpes.

When she disclosed her results, Val was disappointed but let Anne know she still wanted to be sexually intimate and talked very specifically about how they could do that with the least risk possible. She felt comfortable being sexual as long as Anne was taking Valtrex and not having any symptoms of an outbreak. Neither of them was interested in using dental dams, although Anne said she was willing to, if that's what Val wanted. They continued with their plans and went away the following weekend— and enjoyed themselves tremendously, in a full sexual way. Anne still felt sad about having herpes but felt grateful that she and Val had bonded around the decision to face it together.

Another thing that helped Anne was when she confided in Judy, a friend she admired and trusted. Judy's response was, "I've had herpes for years. Want to help me start a support group?" Judy said she believed the way to destigmatize herpes was to be more public about it instead of keeping it as a shameful secret.

Public health workers would probably be very supportive of Judy's idea. When compared with the actual level of public health risk, herpes

>

gets an inordinate amount of attention, perhaps because it is so prevalent and incurable. As a result much of their valuable time, energy, and
resources are devoted to helping people with the social stigma attached
to herpes, an infection is very common and that usually does not have
any serious medical consequences. In fact, for this very reason, many doctors and public health workers are reluctant to even test for herpes unless
there are signs of an outbreak.[C]

Though it was especially awkward to find out right before that first
trip, in retrospect, Anne was grateful she found out when she did. "Thank
goodness I found out before I had sex with her," she said. "Imagine how
it would feel if we'd started a relationship and *then* I found out?" This way
Val had informed consent. If despite their precautions Val did become
infected, she couldn't blame Anne for not telling her.

A few months later, Anne realized that she and Val didn't feel enough
emotional connection for a long-term commitment to each other. They
parted ways peacefully and have remained on friendly terms. What struck
Anne later was that she could have felt trapped in the relationship by guilt
because she had exposed Val to herpes. Instead, their honest communication
about herpes helped both of them feel free to evaluate their relationship on
more important criteria, such as their emotional "fit" with each other.

WHEN WE FOLLOW these rules, guidelines, and techniques, we can
become aware of our habitual defenses and destructive patterns,
and genuine understanding begins to blossom. You'll be richly
rewarded with your partner's gratitude and trust, and you'll learn
valuable information that will help both of you reach a resolution.
Each time you succeed in communicating about a challenging issue,
your trust and love will deepen, making each new challenge easier
and easier to face together.

Your Turn

① Before you can be honest with someone else, you have to be able to be honest with yourself. Have you recognized and come to terms with what is and isn't sexually pleasing for you? Do you know what turns you on the most or helps you have orgasms? Are you honest with yourself about how much you enjoy certain sexual acts that may please your partner? Or are you trying to talk yourself into believing that you enjoy something when you really don't?

② Write down, for your eyes only, your responses to the questions above about what helps you feel more turned on, have orgasms, etc. Write every request as an I-statement, and make it positive: "I like it when you do this . . . and I wish you'd do that more. . . ." If you catch yourself drifting into you-statements or criticisms, stop and rewrite until you can get a positive I-statement. It may take time! When you've checked and double-checked, to be sure you have positive I-statements, ask yourself if you think you and your partner could do this exercise together. If you think so, then ask her to read this section and see if wants to write her answers down too. If she does, that's great. If she doesn't, wait a few days before you decide if you want to pursue this any more. Even if you don't do this specific exercise with her, you can still benefit from practicing how to phrase your requests as positive I-statements.

③ Look for opportunities to practice a little active listening with your partner, on any topic, without telling her that's what you're doing. For instance, if she says she had a rough day at work, see if you can reflect her feelings enough to get her to tell you more. Check inside yourself to see if you can really put yourself in her shoes and understand how she's feeling. Pay attention to how you feel while you're doing that. More connected? Interested? Irritated? Bored? Curious?

④ If you could choose just one sexual behavior to talk with your partner about, what would it be? It's important not to overwhelm someone with a long list of demands. What's one thing that would make a positive difference for you? Can you think of a good time to bring that up with her?

10

The Secret of 24-Hour Foreplay

FOR YEARS, I have been fascinated by learning more about a certain subgroup of queer women who have been seriously overlooked. After reading this chapter, I think you will be intrigued and curious about them as well. The women I'm talking about are still sexually active with their partners, even after ten years together.

In the infamous 1983 Blumstein and Schwartz survey (mentioned in previous chapters) that identified lesbian couples as the sexual-loss leaders, there was a fascinating subgroup who didn't get nearly as much attention. Among women living together for ten years or more, 20 percent said they still had sex at least twice a month.[1] And then in the online survey I conducted in 2007, there was that 20 percent again—couples, living together more than ten years, who had sex twice a month or more. That's the inspirational group, the antidote to depressing "bed death" news.

What do you suppose they have that the other 80 percent don't? True love, the likes of which most of us will never experience? Perfect bodies? Supreme self-confidence? Sky-high levels of testosterone in their bloodstreams? Do they live carefree lives with few responsibilities, plenty of free time, and zero emotional baggage? Or maybe these women are just incredibly, irresistibly hot throughout their lives?

Actually, none of these explains why some couples stay sexually active (SA) while others let their intimacy fade away. Thank goodness. If these were the criteria for long-lasting intimacy, we'd all be out of luck! No, the women of these SA long-term couples deal with the same problems and insecurities we all do. Yet despite this, they manage to keep sexual energy flourishing for years on end, for one simple reason: They understand the power and necessity of 24-hour foreplay.

Now for many people, the word "foreplay" refers to physical stimulation before proceeding to the sexual "main event." That's not what I mean. Twenty-four hours of *that* kind of foreplay, of course, would be far from pleasurable . . . and probably unbearable.

Remember chapter 2, where I described the behavioral factors associated with limerence, the state of falling in love? Those things we "find ourselves doing" when we're head over heels, such as setting aside time to be relaxed and alone together, taking special care of our bodies and appearance, creating a sensual atmosphere? Well, that golden 20 percent of SA couples are successful because they purposefully and consciously re-create those conditions of limerence using intentional planning and behavior. That's what I mean by 24-hour foreplay.

"Ugh! That seems too contrived!" If that's your first reaction, you're not alone. Many women have an instant aversion to the idea of planning for sex. But it's *not about planning for sex*—it's about planning time to connect with each other in a way that makes you want to be sexual. In other words, it's about planning foreplay.

That said, foreplay is not just a means to an end. When it comes to strengthening and deepening intimacy, 24-hour foreplay is not just a precursor to sex. In many ways, it *is* "the main event." Sharing positive emotional and sensual and erotic feelings can only improve your intimate connection with each other. Much of the time, that itself will lead you into making love. Other times it won't, but you'll have a very enjoyable 24 hours.

Not everyone can see this right away. In one intimacy workshop, when we were talking about the importance of fostering an emotional connection during 24-hour foreplay, someone said "You mean I have to *think* about her?" Her partner turned to her and dryly remarked, "Yes, but not all the time. Just twenty-four hours before you want sex. The rest of the time, you can be yourself."

This hilarious exchange actually conveyed a valid point. Just because "24-hour" is in the name doesn't mean you have to think about sex for 24 hours *straight*; it's more like starting to think about it 24 hours in advance. And there's no reason it should feel like a chore. If that sentiment starts to come up in my workshops, and it often does, I ask everyone to take five minutes to recall what they used to do to prepare for a hot date with a new lover. And then a light bulb goes on. Almost unanimously, the women are surprised to realize that they were practicing foreplay when they thought they were just falling in love.

Now it's your turn. Think about how you acted when you first got intimately involved with your partner. Try to remember how you got ready for an evening with her. Did you think of ways to make it romantic? Did you arrange for privacy? Did you pay extra attention to making your body feel good, by doing things like exercising or taking hot baths or doing yoga? Did you choose something to wear that looked good on you? Did you have fresh sheets on the bed in case you brought her home? Did you imagine how it would feel to kiss and hold her, or visualize sexual scenes, or re-live recent encounters with her in your mind? Did you have these thoughts hours, or even days, before your date?

If you did, guess what? You were practicing 24-hour foreplay. Consciously or not, you were building positive anticipation for your next sexual opportunity, and as a result, you were creating sexual desire. And it was fun, wasn't it?

Bonnie and Cathy contacted me when a friend told them about my research study on lesbian sexual patterns. "I'll bet she'd love to talk with you. You guys have something special." The friend was right: I did enjoy talking with them, and they really did have something special.

They were both almost fifty years old and had just celebrated their 20th anniversary when we first talked. In response to my preliminary questions, they described a satisfying sexual relationship, saying they usually made love two or three times a month. They suspected that they were more sexually active than most of their friends, although they said it was hard to know, because no one really talked about it. When I confirmed that yes, they were more active than most long-term lesbian couples, Cathy said, "I thought so!" Then she added, "That makes me feel good, but in a way I feel sad for them, because they're missing out on something so special."

I scheduled separate telephone interviews with each of them so that I could hear their individual perspectives on sexual intimacy privately. I was impressed with how much they respected each other, how similar they were in valuing sexual intimacy.

>

Before she met Bonnie, Cathy was a "well-read virgin." She was shy, but Bonnie was patient, and they made love about two months after meeting. Cathy described it as a wonderful, fulfilling, "coming home to myself" experience that forever sealed her bond with Bonnie. Twenty years later, she still appreciated Bonnie for "bringing me out and keeping me out." But after their first year together, she noticed a decline in their sexual frequency, and she panicked. She said she was afraid that Bonnie had gotten tired of her inexperience and wanted to find someone more like herself. She talked with Bonnie, who assured her that she was a wonderful lover and that a little less sex was to be expected at this point. Cathy said she relaxed as time passed, and she noticed they still had sex regularly, just not as frequently as before. She felt relieved to know that Bonnie valued sexual intimacy as much as she did, even when neither was feeling particularly turned on or "in the mood."

But Bonnie and Cathy didn't become passive about their sexual intimacy. Though they knew it was normal for frequency to drop off somewhat as time went on, they also knew that without some cultivation, their intimacy could wither away. So they both took steps to address this. As a systems analyst, Cathy was a natural pragmatist. She began to read articles about how to keep sexual energy flowing in a long-term relationship. She started to pay attention to things that helped get her more turned on sexually. In general, Cathy took longer to get warmed up than Bonnie did. But instead of judging herself about that, she used that difference to help herself. She would start making love to Bonnie first, and then she noticed that she would get sexually aroused when she felt Bonnie responding to her stimulation.

There were some obstacles. A few years after they began living together, Cathy started having fluctuations in her weight, gaining and losing 70 pounds several times. When she was at a higher weight, Cathy felt more self-conscious and wondered whether Bonnie was still attracted to

>

her. When they talked about this, Bonnie reassured her that she loved her voluptuousness. "In twenty years," Cathy said, "Bonnie has never said anything critical about my weight. She's helped me with food plans when I asked her to, but she's never suggested or hinted that I should lose weight, or tied that to us being sexual with each other."

What Bonnie did suggest was that Cathy begin practicing yoga as a way to learn to love her body more. Cathy did, and she found that it did great things for her. "It's a way I can really feel myself physically, appreciate what my arms and legs do for me, and be inside my body instead of outside, judging myself," she said. Focusing on the physical sensations in her body during yoga helped her feel more grounded, relaxed, and sensual. Later, Cathy noticed that the good feelings from yoga often carried over for one or two days. She began taking her yoga class on Fridays so she could start the weekend feeling better about herself physically. The good feelings rolled over into Saturday's time for sexual intimacy.

When I asked if there was anything else she'd like to add, Cathy hesitated, then laughed. "Well, I don't know how other people feel about this, but sometimes there are movies or books that turn me on, you know what I mean?" I assured her that I did know what she meant, and that many other women enjoy erotica. She seemed relieved to hear this, and continued. "Sometimes we've ordered videos to watch together . . . and I have some books that are a turn-on for me, so sometimes I'll read some before we're going to have sex. Maybe even the day before. It gives me some fantasy material. I used to feel guilty about this, but Bonnie told me she likes it too, so that helped. I don't always tell her I'm doing it. I figure she doesn't care how I get there as long as I'm into it when we're together."

When I talked with Bonnie, it was clear that she placed a high value on sexual intimacy in her life with Cathy. "You have to make it a priority, and put it on your schedule. If you don't schedule it, it won't happen. Life

>

is too busy, and other things get in the way." Both women had demanding jobs, and both had some responsibility for aging parents who lived in the same city and often needed assistance. In addition to those responsibilities, Bonnie and Cathy were avid hikers and enjoyed a wide network of friends. They had very full lives.

But Bonnie didn't let that stand in the way of a regular rendezvous with Cathy. "We try to save one weekend morning for just us," she said. "We're both morning people; I'd just fall asleep if we tried it at night. It might be Saturday or Sunday morning, maybe just a couple hours, but enough time to chill out a little bit together." During this time they avoided telephone calls, emails, and visits from family or friends. Bonnie stressed, "You can't always guarantee you'll have sex, but at least you can block off some private time and see what happens. It's good for us to reconnect that way."

Bonnie and Cathy understood that it takes time to get into a sexual frame of mind, and that you have to be deliberate about it. This was the key to their vibrant sexual relationship. Each one seemed to take responsibility for her own sexuality, and they also worked together as a team to protect their privacy and time for intimacy. They identified activities that helped build sexual desire and arousal, and they deliberately focused on these *before* a sexual encounter.

In other words, they practiced 24-hour foreplay.

I remember one workshop in which a woman talked about her "date panties." She said knew she was preparing to sleep with her new girlfriend when she chose her favorite panties to wear on a date. "You know, you want to look good when you take your clothes off," she laughed. She also described other things she did to get ready for her date: cleaned the house, changed the sheets, selected background music, lit candles, and told her friends not to call. All of this felt exciting to her—not awkward and contrived, and not like a chore.

Now, I'm well aware of how life changes when you get settled in a relationship. But it isn't really that life changes—we change. With relative stability in our love lives, we tend to let work, family, school, and other factors encroach on our free time. It's like we think, *Now that I don't have to impress her any more, I can focus on* real *life*. But there are two critical errors with that thought: First, this *is* real life, and second, we all want to be impressive, we're just afraid of feeling foolish.

When I say "this *is* real life," I mean that time doesn't stand still, living organisms don't stop changing, free time is always in short supply, and there are always choices to be made. If you like to garden, you know what I mean. After you get that first beautiful batch of fresh flowers, you don't usually say, "Phew! Garden's done; let's focus on something else." On the contrary—you may rededicate yourself to weeding and watering, so new flowers keep blooming to replace the ones that fade and drop off. Your garden won't stand still any more than the rest of your life or your relationships. Constant changes, constant needs.

The second point goes a little deeper. Everyone wants to impress—it's human nature, and it's a good thing. Impressing someone makes us proud, but the flip side of pride is shame. The same energy that goes into pumping up a good image can turn on a dime, going straight into feeling foolish and wondering, *Why did I even try?* It's much easier at the beginning of a relationship. She doesn't really know you yet and has no idea how hard you're trying. It's later, after you know each other very well, that you're more vulnerable. It makes sense that practicing foreplay could feel awkward and contrived: You're trying, she knows it, and it might not work. No wonder you feel "too busy"!

If this rings true for you, remember to be compassionate and realistic. It takes courage to take chances, so give yourself credit when you do. And also remember that the rest of your life doesn't grind to a halt when you move into foreplay mode. You just need to make a little space in your day and in your mind. You can even multitask with foreplay, drifting into a sexual image while driving to the grocery store, remembering how her breasts feel. You can even practice tightening and relaxing your vaginal muscles while you're having your coffee break. I know you have to get back to work, but believe me, work will be more enlivening when you have a little extra charge going on.

Have you noticed that much of 24-hour foreplay is a solitary activity? That's important to notice, because it reminds us that we can't expect our partners to turn us on. We have to turn on ourselves. In the early 1970s, feminist writer Robin Morgan urged women to "Take responsibility for your own orgasm!" In the same way, you also need to take responsibility for your own arousal. After all, you're the one who knows better than anyone else what carries you onto a sexual wavelength, so you're the best person for the job of getting yourself there.

Most of us have a set of conditions that help us get turned on. For some women, the conditions can be general, such as, "I just need a day alone and an hour of exercise." For others, the conditions are more specific, almost as if all the planets have to be lined up correctly. In a recent workshop, one woman said, "Everything has to be just so. The lights need to be low—no music playing, because that's distracting; one glass of wine to relax—but not two, or I'll go to sleep. If the telephone rings, that will disturb the mood, or if she brings up anything about work, forget it." She paused, with a questioning look on her face, and asked, "Is it that hard for everyone?" We all laughed a little together, but she found she was not alone. The fact is, there's no "right" or "wrong" or "normal" or "weird" way to get turned on. Whatever works, works. Embrace it, and use it.

As I said earlier, 24-hour foreplay is primarily a solitary activity. But if your partner happens to be around, you can make use of that fact too. You can make more eye contact with her, or let yourself smile more, or touch her affectionately. If you like what she's wearing, compliment her . . . or simply really *look* at what it is you're liking. However, don't feel as if you need to be a skilled flirt all over again, or that you need to be a seductress. That can be paralyzing, because it puts too much pressure on you *and* on your partner's response. Instead, just be present to what is really happening for you in the moment.

This is a challenge for many of us, and it's a really important point. We're usually thinking about what's already happened or what's coming next, rarely sensing what's going on right now. If you're not present, you won't notice the sensual responses you're having before your attention goes back to your boss, or picking up the kids from school, or what to make for that dinner party tomorrow night. You may miss this moment, and then later wonder why you let it slip past you.

With today's hectic lifestyle, being fully present is particularly challenging. But there is an almost surefire shortcut: tuning into your senses. Pick one of the five senses and contemplate only what you are "picking up" with that sense. For example, try to listen to everything that can be heard: the ticking of your watch, the turning of a page, the honking of a horn, the barking of the neighbor's dog. Try to listen to the sound entirely, but without "interpreting" by giving it a story (such as, "The dog is barking because the neighbors leave it alone too much."). Just hear. Or you might tune into sensations in the body. Where are you tense? Where do you feel like stretching? As you practice and develop this skill of paying attention to one physical sense, you'll find yourself better able to be present, centered, and calm.

Felicia had been with Treena for nineteen years. They had two children and rarely took time for a date, much less sex. It had been two years since they had been sexually intimate. Felicia said, "I just never feel the urge any more." Treena wanted more intimacy, but she refused to initiate because she'd already been turned down too many times. She felt alternately hurt and angry. Felicia was afraid that Treena was near the end of her rope and decided she had to do something.

For several months, Felicia had been questioning her relationship. At times she wanted to be free to explore other possibilities and people, and at other times she knew she needed stability for herself and her children. She hadn't felt "in love" with Treena for a long time and wondered if that could happen again—with anyone. Felicia also felt extremely anxious at work and worried constantly about not measuring up to her high-profile

>

---

management position. At some point she realized that her professional frustrations were spilling over into her relationship with Treena. She hadn't been feeling much self-love at the office and realized that might be interfering with her ability to feel loving toward her partner. When she sorted through these feelings, Felicia decided to try to be sexual again with Treena. She wanted to know if this might help them feel closer and might even help her feel better about herself. She could remember some very positive sexual experiences in the past, and this helped motivate her to try again.

Although she seemed more positive about wanting their relationship to improve, Felicia also had some reservations. Would sexual intimacy make her feel more trapped? What if it didn't go well—would she feel like a failure? In spite of these questions, she was willing to make an effort. She planned a romantic weekend in a city they both loved to celebrate Treena's birthday. Three weeks in advance, she arranged for the children to stay with their grandparents on the birthday weekend. She researched online and reserved a room at an upscale hotel. She also made dinner reservations and found a nearby music club. When Felicia presented this plan, Treena seemed mildly interested and said it would be nice to get away, but she made no comment about anything romantic or sexual. Treena had been disappointed before.

Felicia felt very pessimistic as the weekend approached. She said Treena seemed unenthusiastic and she feared that neither of them would be "in the mood." She also knew that she would have to initiate sex and was afraid that she couldn't get aroused herself. However, she was determined to see this through to the bitter end, so she could say, "At least I tried."

Because she seemed so pessimistic, I asked Felicia how she might sabotage the whole weekend if she wanted to. Like most people, she objected to this idea, saying she had worked hard to arrange everything. However, when pressed, she had no trouble identifying two things that

>

would ensure that sex did not happen. One would be to start talking about her family. Treena felt very slighted by them, and discussions about the family usually ended badly. Even though both would say they were trying to resolve the issues, this never happened. Instead, Treena would wind up feeling hurt, Felicia would feel guilty, and both would feel more distant from each other. Sex would never happen after such a discussion.

The other thing Felicia predicted could sabotage the weekend would be to eat and drink too much. She sometimes told herself a glass of wine helped her "loosen up" for sex, but instead what happened would be that she would have two glasses and then get sleepy and numb. She was sure that more than one glass of wine would completely wipe out the benefits of all the preparation she had done. This was especially pertinent because Felicia wanted to go listen to music after dinner, so there would be plenty of food, alcohol, and late hours to compete with time and energy for sexual intimacy.

So how did the weekend go? Felicia glowed as she described it. Treena told her, "This was the best birthday I ever had." They relaxed in the hotel spa, went walking and window-shopping, ordered room service on the balcony, and chatted for hours. Felicia talked to Treena about her career struggles. Treena talked about lingering grief she felt from her mother's death the year before. They both laughed about how great it was to be away from their children.

Then they made love, and Felicia was amazed. She said, "It was all just so easy and spontaneous. Like it used to be."

Spontaneous? After three weeks of detailed planning? More like extensive, extended foreplay!

The magical weekend happened because 1) Felicia decided to make her best effort, and 2) she was conscious of what could sabotage the weekend—and she chose not to do those things. During their weekend, Felicia had several urges to bring up loaded family topics, and she also considered an extra glass of wine with dinner. Having identified these as turn-offs, she caught those impulses and chose not to respond to them.

Several months later, Felicia was still pleased about how she had handled the weekend. She was also still surprised at how easily she could sabotage efforts to get closer to Treena, and how empowered she felt by knowing that she could choose not to do that. She and Treena had made love several times since the weekend. They were thankful to have broken the long dry spell and felt a renewal of their connection to each other. They also understood, and talked about, their need to be mindful and keep planning regular opportunities for sexual contact. Most of all, they appreciated each other's commitment to enriching their intimate relationship.

Another way to redirect attention to your physical senses is with yoga or exercise. Feeling good in your skin is an important part of feeling sensual, and most women find it particularly helpful to attend to their bodies before attempting to have a sexual connection. Yoga is a unique opportunity to deliberately focus awareness on what you feel in your body, appreciating the tension and relaxation, movement and stillness. Vigorous exercise helps in some different ways. Endorphins can give you a rush of good feelings, and building muscles makes you feel stronger and more capable. The important thing is to focus on what you feel in your body. Foreplay exercise is about loving and appreciating your body, not about looking good. In fact, if you get distracted with body-image worries, exercise becomes nonproductive, so switch to yoga or something else that keeps you in a mode of sensual awareness. Feeling good in your skin is what helps you feel better about a sexual connection.

I've been talking about the positive behaviors of foreplay. Now it's time to address something equally important: self-sabotage, or how to make sure sex doesn't actually happen even when you say you want it. Sometimes things happen that you can't control—the heating-and-air repair person shows up hours earlier or later than you expected, a tree falls on your house, your boss gives you an urgent project to finish before tomorrow. But for the most part, we do the damage ourselves. Most of us have a little self-defeating streak that emerges whenever we want to do something good for ourselves. You may know what's good for you or your relationship, and yet you find yourself doing the opposite. You may bring your partner to a lovely, romantic setting and then start an argument that completely ruins the ambience. Afterward, people often say, "Something just hit me wrong." But why did it hit you wrong at precisely that moment? That's the more interesting question.

When I first talk about self-sabotage, most people look confused. "Why would I want to do that?" I don't know why we humans are like this, but I certainly believe the conflict is universal. Freud might have explained it as the "death instinct" at war with life and growth. Other explanations could be that we need to maintain homeostasis by not making major life changes, or that the "old and familiar" is safer than the "new and unknown." Existential humanists talk about the conflict between growth and safety, or isolation and connection. The very fact that there are so many explanations for this ubiquitous phenomenon tells you how universal it is.

Fortunately, just because it's a universal conflict doesn't mean you're doomed to forever shoot yourself in the foot. Here's the great weapon you have: conscious awareness. If you pay attention to how you might defeat yourself, chances are you won't. Once you're conscious of something, it can't happen unconsciously. This is why therapists often ask couples to predict how they might start a fight with each other. Most of us know exactly how to do that, because we know each other's buttons. Knowing this ahead of time lets you choose your direction. If you want to create a positive sexual experience, you can do that by practicing foreplay. If you need to work some other things out first, you can do that too, by talking with your partner. But what you don't need to do is to blow up a sexual opportunity just to avoid being sexual. You'll feel much better if you talk about your conflicts openly instead of acting them out through self-sabotage.

Harville Hendrix, the author of several books—including the classic *Getting the Love You Want*—talks about the difference between conscious and unconscious marriage. By this he means that until we become aware of how our own family dynamics are impacting our relationships, we act them out unconsciously. We can be conscious in our relationships when we acknowledge the needs and influences from our past that are shaping our current relationships. Again, once you're conscious of something, you won't act it out unconsciously.

To me, foreplay and self-sabotage are like conscious and unconscious intimacy. I can use my rational mind to learn about myself and my partner, and intentionally use that knowledge to facilitate sexual intimacy between us. That's a conscious choice. Or I can remain unconscious of my potential for self-sabotage, and act that out instead. Trust me, conscious intimacy feels better.

Your Turn

① Try to finish the following incomplete sentences. Be sure to write your answers down! You'll be surprised at what a difference it make to write these down instead of just thinking them. Also, if your partner is interested, give her these instructions and let her write her own responses. *Do not read each other's written responses!* After you've finished this exercise separately, you may want to read some of what you wrote to your partner, and let her do the same—but that's your choice. If you start this exercise knowing that your partner will read it, you're going to edit too much and you won't get the full benefits.

- Some things I do to help me get in a sexual mood are:

  _____.

- Some things my partner does that help me get in a sexual mood are:

  _____.

- Some things I do to try to help my partner get in a sexual mood are:

  _____.

- If I wanted to sabotage a sexual opportunity, I could always:

  _____.

- Sometimes we both do things to sabotage sexual opportunities. For example, I remember when we:

  _____.

11

Igniting Your Erotic Imagination

WHAT IS "EROTIC imagination"? The only way to answer that question accurately is to be very general: It includes *any* mental images or thoughts that are sexually stimulating.

Contrary to what many women believe, enjoying your own erotic imagination does *not* take anything away from your partner. On the contrary, your imagination is a wonderful way to bring your most private, sexy thoughts to your most intimate connection, that is, to your partner. It's where we can integrate the human polarities of sex: that of the deep, loving, soulful bond and that of a primitive, lustful, self-oriented drive.

Erotic imagination can be romantic and innocuous, such as the vision of a lover's breasts, the memory of a kiss, or the feeling of dancing close together. Thinking about how her arms feel around you is a form of erotic imagination. So is thinking about how it feels to touch her hair. Dreaming about how the two of you may finally be together can be a sexual fantasy too. These forms of erotic imagination don't usually cause much guilt, because desire for a beloved partner feels congruent with romantic ideals of loving, intimate relationship. Not so for the "dirty" or "forbidden" taboo fantasies that may surprise and even trouble us. In contrast to themes of longing and anticipation, "naughty" scenarios seem crass, wrong, immoral. Feelings of lust, aggression, power, revenge—all of these "bad" urges are present in these kinds of erotic scenarios. These are the kinds of fantasies that women write about on anonymous surveys or confess in very private conversations. They're not nice, respectful, or loving—more like primitive or selfish. Though such fantasies are common and are absolutely no indicator of any psychological issues, women who get turned on by "the dark stuff" often worry that they are deficient, morally and psychologically.

Suzanne, a sixty-year old attorney, came out in her late 30s. Before then, she had been married to a man. During her heterosexual years, Suzanne had orgasms less than half of the time when she had sex. Every time she made love, she worried that "it might not happen." Sometimes, she said, she would avoid sex because she thought she would end up feeling frustrated and inadequate. She finally, with much embarrassment, talked to her therapist, who suggested she read Nancy Friday's *My Secret Garden*. It changed her sex life forever.

Suzanne was amazed and thrilled to discover how turned on she got by reading other women's fantasies. Plus, it was a huge relief for her to realize that having these kinds of thoughts and images was apparently normal and healthy, and that there's usually no correlation between what you like in fantasy and in reality. Ever since she discovered masturbation as a teenager, she'd been carrying guilt about a very specific, detailed fantasy that would bring her to orgasm very quickly. She had felt very guilty about masturbating at all, and about indulging in such dirty thoughts. Suzanne developed a nightly ritual, which became the way she compromised between giving in to her sexual urges and believing that they were

>

wrong. She would fantasize, masturbate, have an orgasm, feel guilty, and promise herself she wouldn't do it again. The next night she would repeat this cycle. This compromise worked for several years. After Suzanne went to college and began sharing a dorm room, she stopped masturbating so regularly and forgot all about her compromise with fantasy and guilt. She also forgot about how powerful that fantasy could be in getting her to arousal and orgasm. After reading *My Secret Garden,* the memory of the fantasy came back to her.

"I used to have this fantasy about being forced to have sex with several men," she told me. "I felt terribly ashamed and wondered what was wrong with me, but I kept using that fantasy when I masturbated, because I'd get so excited and have such intense orgasms. Of course, I couldn't ask anyone else about it. It felt like my dirty secret. But then, reading this book, I realized this was pretty normal, and that it could help me enjoy sex with my husband more. I tried it, and it worked!"

For Suzanne, using fantasy to have an orgasm was a bridge to a more satisfying sexual relationship. She could now channel her erotic imagination, and that became an important part of her personal foreplay. She said, "Instead of worrying about having an orgasm, or hoping he'd touch me exactly the way I needed, I could help myself come by concentrating on a fantasy. It made me start enjoying sex more, and looking forward to it more. I didn't tell him exactly what I was doing, but I'm sure he could tell something was different, because I relaxed a lot more."

Her discovery also helped her understand her partner's use of erotic imagination instead of being threatened by it. "My husband used to get an erotic magazine. At first, I took it personally: *Does that mean he's not satisfied with me?* But then I discovered that I'd get turned on reading parts of the magazine, and it helped me get more in the mood for sex. I felt more in control. I knew it would help me get turned on and ready to have sex. I'm lucky he didn't try to hide those magazines from me!"

>

As Suzanne continued to relax her attitude toward erotic imagination, she started really paying attention to what she responded to sexually. This is when her attraction to women began to surface.

"This may seem strange, because after I started having more orgasms during sex with my husband, I also started thinking I might be gay. It was confusing, because I liked fantasizing about both men and women. At first I thought that must mean I'm bisexual. Then I noticed that, in real life, I was looking at women a lot more than I looked at men. I was in law school then, and most of my friends were men, but I just didn't have much sexual interest in them. Then a woman joined our study group, and I felt a surge of sexual interest that shocked me. That was the beginning of the end of my heterosexual life."

Ironically, the incentive of a more enjoyable sex life with her husband motivated Suzanne to keep working through guilt and confusion about all aspects of her sexuality, and ended up giving her the freedom to claim her true sexual orientation. Erotic imagination served as a catalyst for her. She continues to enjoy this life-changing discovery.

"After I came out and began having sexual relationships with women, I continued to use sexual fantasy as a way to get more turned on. I wasn't sure whether I should tell my partners I did this. I was afraid they would think I wasn't really gay because my fantasies included men and penises, not just women. Lucky for me, I met women who were very open and matter-of-fact about fantasy."

Today, Suzanne is in a satisfying monogamous relationship with a woman who understands her use of erotic imagination and doesn't mind that it includes both genders, and even some taboo subjects. She loves the unconflicted feeling of control she has over her arousal, and she is more sexually confident than she has ever been.

In 1978, Nancy Friday interviewed dozens of women, asking them about their favorite sexual fantasies. She published these in her book, *My Secret Garden*, a collection of fantasies that include acts of domination, submission, degradation, group sex, forced sex, anonymous sex, exhibitionism, voyeurism, and bestiality, among others. Her book was a breakthrough for many women. It eased the guilt for many women who had already discovered the power of their erotic imagination, and it encouraged others to dip into their own personal reservoirs. In discussing her findings, Friday observed that deliberate use of fantasy helps women feel more in control of their own sexual responses. She also emphasized that most of the things women fantasize about are things they would never actually *want* to do.

Many women feel sexually empowered by their use of erotic imagination, knowing they can facilitate arousal and orgasm by tapping into this internal reservoir of stimulating thoughts and images. But not surprisingly, for some women, erotic imagination is often a raging source of chronic inner conflict, a continual cycle of push/pull. They're pulled by secret "dirty thoughts" that transport them to more intense sexual excitement, but they're pushed by feelings of guilt and shame. Or they're pulled with the knowledge that having fantasies is healthy but pushed by fear when their fantasies involve situations that seem morally or psychologically unhealthy.

What is missing amid all this inner conflict is the fact that erotic imagination is a gift! It's a gift to be enjoyed privately, and sometimes even shared with a partner. It's a gift because it's a vital component of sexual foreplay, arousal, and orgasm, and it can be enjoyed privately or sometimes even shared with a partner. It's a gift because it gives us a sense of familiarity with our sexual selves, which only enhances what we bring to partner sex. And it's a gift because it gives us a sense of privacy and separateness, which we need in order be sexually present and vulnerable.

The fact is, most women need more than one source of stimulation to get aroused and reach orgasm, and that stimulation is not always physical. It can also come from a variety of other sources: your partner's words, looking at things that turn you on, focusing on your internal sexual fantasies. In fact, in the moments just before orgasm, most people are not focusing on their partner; they're focusing on internal erotic thoughts and images.[1]

This may not fit with some women's romantic ideals, but like it or not, it does fit with what most women say is actually going on mentally when they are having sexual contact. Some women find this upsetting, thinking it smacks of disloyalty: "But you shouldn't have to fantasize if you're really in love!" After all, sexual contact is "supposed to" be the expression of a deeply loving, intimate bond between two people who are committed to each other. To women who feel strongly about this, the internal focus on one's private, erotic imagination seems selfish, shallow, or threatening to their "real world" sexual connection. But there is no evidence at all that having fantasies takes away from the richness of your sex life. On the contrary, it seems to help. Research shows about 85 percent of women fantasize at least some of the time during sex with a partner, and that that those who fantasize more also enjoy sex more: They report more satisfaction, more orgasms, less guilt, and fewer sexual difficulties than people who fantasize less.[2]

Vivian called me to ask if she and Melinda could come talk about sexual intimacy issues. They had been seeing a therapist for couples' counseling and were feeling better about many issues. But their therapist had suggested they might benefit from a consultation about their sex life. They agreed and scheduled a session. When they came in, both of them agreed that they had a very specific problem that was the source of a lot of conflict between them. Looking embarrassed, Vivian said she had to engage in a specific fantasy in order to have an orgasm. Since she began masturbating as a teenager, Vivian liked to fantasize that a man was restraining her and pressing his full weight on her body. When she was making love, Vivian liked for Melinda to emulate this by covering her with pillows and lying across her body. She was very ashamed that she needed this kind of stimulation.

Although she participated reluctantly, Melinda had multiple objections to this. First of all, she thought that fantasizing during sex was unhealthy, since lovers should be completely focused on each other. Melinda placed a very high value on a sense of spiritual and romantic connection with her partner. She said she had been with other lovers with whom she felt completely merged and "lost in each other," and thought this was the ideal. To her, it was impossible to have that kind of connection when you were absorbed in a sexual fantasy. It also bothered Melinda that Vivian fantasized about being overpowered by a man. She interpreted this to mean that Vivian was conflicted about being lesbian, and that she had unresolved power and control issues. Melinda thought Vivian should go to individual therapy to work out her problems so she wouldn't bring these into their sex life. At a deeper level, Melinda wondered if Vivian was secretly wishing she were with a man instead of with her. No wonder this bothered her!

We talked about the research evidence, which shows that most women fantasize at least some of the time, that many lesbians have fantasies

>

involving men and penises, and that scenes of domination and submission are very common. We also talked about how there isn't a direct relationship between what you fantasize about and what you want in real life. Vivian was relieved to hear that her fantasy didn't indicate severe pathology that would require years of therapy to overcome.

I asked Vivian if she had ever shared her fantasies with any previous lovers. She said, "No, Melinda's the first person I trusted enough to tell about this. Before her, I kept the fantasy to myself, and I usually didn't have orgasms during sex with my other partners."

This was surprising for Melinda to hear, and it put things in perspective. She realized that Vivian had needed a lot of courage to invite her into this very private realm. It showed her how much she was loved and trusted. It's an honor to be loved and trusted like that!

However, Melinda really wanted those romantic merging feelings during sex. She needed some time to process a new way of thinking about how separate thoughts can enhance sexual connection. But I had high hopes for them when they left. I knew that Melinda's realization would help her to feel included, valued, loved, and trusted. I suspect that this would help turn Vivian's fantasy from a source of threat to a source of bonding—a feeling that was important to Melinda not only romantically but also sexually. After all, Melinda had a fantasy of her own, a physically impossible, though more socially acceptable, one: complete merging during lovemaking. It's possible that once Melinda came to accept Vivian's fantasy, she could also see that their two fantasies weren't necessarily mutually exclusive.

Often people are surprised that so many women indulge in sexual fantasy—and here's another surprise: Numerous studies have demonstrated that women often have automatic and unconscious physiological responses to sexual images. In one study, women in a research lab were hooked up to a tamponlike device called a vaginal photoplethysmograph (VP), which records increases in vaginal lubrication and clitoral engorgement.[3] Then they watched sexually explicit videos. The VP showed that all of the women became lubricated and engorged while watching the videos. Everyone showed physical evidence of sexual arousal.

However, when asked to use a written scale to rate how aroused they were, almost half said they weren't aroused at all. Were they lying, or was there some kind of mind–body disconnect in response to the erotic videos? The evidence suggests that the women were not, in fact, lying. Research shows that physiological arousal can happen unconsciously; that our bodies can respond, even if our minds haven't gone there.

Chances are you've never been hooked up to a VP, so this study may not at first resonate for you personally. But ask yourself whether you've ever discovered you had become lubricated when you weren't conscious of it at the time. A friend of mine once told me, "I was talking to a coworker about our staff meeting. Later I went to the bathroom and realized my panties were wet. Then it hit me that I'd been watching her mouth while we were talking." She was at work, in a "work" frame of mind, and wasn't having any conscious sexual thoughts about the woman. But her body responded nevertheless. It was an automatic sexual response that occurred unconsciously.

Evidence that we all respond to sexually graphic imagery may be disturbing to women who believe pornography is dehumanizing and offensive. Unfortunately, some pornography is extremely degrading of women, and some people fear that this may even encourage sexual violence against women. On the other hand, there isn't any solid evidence that the presence or absence of pornography affects attitudes or behavior toward women. What we can know with certainty is that different women have different sensitivities and perspectives on this issue. It's important to remember that people respond sexually to things they would never, ever do or condone.

The evidence from this study also contradicts a widespread stereotype that women don't respond to visual, erotic stimuli in the same way that men do. Apparently, we do, whether we realize it or not. However, there are some interesting differences between the way that men and women respond to visual stimuli. In another study, four groups—gay and straight men and gay and straight women—were shown erotic videos that featured men, women, or both.[4] Both the gay and the straight women became aroused while viewing images of both nude men and women. However, the straight men responded only to nude women, and the gay men responded only to nude men.

It turns out that our sexuality really is more flexible and fluid than men's. What turns us on does not necessarily determine our sexual orientation. This is an important piece of information for lesbians who are troubled by the fact that they find themselves aroused by erotica and fantasies involving men.

Is there anything that can explain why certain things turn certain individuals on and certain things don't? So far, researchers have come up empty-handed on that one. No one really knows why the erotic brain works the way it does, but it seems to be hardwired and fairly innocuous. There are plenty of psychoanalytic hypotheses—some of them stereotypical and even offensive— but they're unprovable, easily contradicted, and even potentially harmful.

The traditional psychological interpretation is that fantasies represent repressed desires. For example, many women fantasize about being forced to have sex. Some people—including many traditional therapists—explain this fantasy by saying that these women feel ashamed that they have sexual desire and therefore need sex to feel forced in order for it to be "okay." That might be a satisfactory explanation if all women who have this kind of fantasy were also sexually repressed. But that's far from true. Many women who are very open and joyful about their sexual desire enjoy this kind of fantasy too.

Others believe that fantasies provide a way to experience the *opposite* of what one really prefers in real life—this is similar to the notion that dreams represent unconscious efforts to compensate for parts of the self that are overly developed in conscious life. From this perspective, a woman who feels overly responsible and burdened in real life could balance that with a fantasy of being controlled and having to follow orders. If she bought into this kind of misguided interpretation, it might lead her to think that she should change her basically responsible nature.

Still others think fantasies represent an effort to get an erotic charge out of traumatic events in childhood. Let's say a woman had a very domineering father as a child, and that he made her feel bad about herself. From this perspective, by developing a fantasy that involves domination and getting a sexual thrill out of it, she is taking control of the event in her own mind. While this is meant to be an empowering interpretation, it's a risky one. It might be too easy for the woman, or her partner, to think that meant she "enjoyed" a negative experience. She didn't really, and most people don't, regardless of what they fantasize about.

Ellen, a university chemistry professor, had been with her partner for four-teen years and had sex about once every six months. She came to see me by herself, saying that she couldn't talk freely about her concerns with her partner present. Ellen wished they were more sexually active with each other but felt helpless to change that. After we talked about different issues, I asked her if she used sexual fantasy during masturbation and sex.

Ellen was puzzled. "What do you mean 'during sex'?"

"Many women use fantasies to help them feel more aroused and to reach orgasm," I explained. "They do it whether they're masturbating or with a partner."

Now Ellen was shocked and disgusted. "Why would you need to do that if you're with someone you love and want to be with? That reminds me of my ex-husband. I never knew what he was thinking about when we had sex, but it sure didn't feel like it was *me*. I just felt like a convenient place for him to get off. It didn't even feel that personal. That's what felt so different about being with women. It felt so loving and passionate, like we were really being present with each other. I would hate to think my partner was off in her head thinking about someone else."

It may be surprising, but Ellen's beliefs about sex and fantasy are actually still very common. This way of thinking is very consistent with women's tendency to focus on the concepts of relationship and soul con-nection. Many women crave a mutual passionate connection during sex, what you might feel gazing into your lover's eyes during intense arousal and orgasm. The desire is for complete merging, losing yourself in another

>

person, soaring off together into celestial heights of ecstasy. Fantasizing while having sex seems in conflict with these ideals.

I told Ellen about the research that had been done in this field, showing the correlation between use of fantasy, more sex, and more sexual satisfaction. Ellen was still skeptical, but it was clear that her scientific curiosity had gained a foothold.

"That's so surprising," she said. "I wonder if my partner fantasizes. I've never asked her that, but I'm going to."

It struck me that Ellen didn't know her partner's feelings about this— but then, after some thought, it made sense. After all, she held very firm beliefs about love and sex, and about what is "healthy" sexual behavior. Even if her partner felt differently, it would probably be difficult for her to talk with Ellen about feelings and thoughts that didn't fit in that rigid framework.

Her surprise, and curiosity, led me to ask her if she could bring her partner for a session and let me help them talk more freely with each other. She agreed, and the two of them came in a few weeks later. During their very open, nonjudgmental conversation, Ellen learned that her partner had a vivid erotic imagination which she had been keeping to herself because she knew Ellen would be critical. As they talked about these topics that had been hidden and separate, they felt more open and connected. They also laughed about going home "to discuss this further." At the end of the session, Ellen very thoughtfully acknowledged that her ideals of love and passion may have been interfering with real sexual intimacy.

All of these psychological interpretations of sexual fantasy can be very interesting and completely fictitious. Any of them could be true—or not. For all we know, fantasies are based on random events that happen to be sexually stimulating, for unknown reasons.

There's no evidence that women who enjoy restraint and domination fantasies are afraid of men, dominating in daily life, or reacting to traumatic events in their past. The danger is that misguided and misinformed psychological interpretations can make women feel ashamed of something that's a perfectly normal, potentially helpful mental activity.

In the privacy of your own imagination, you can experiment outside the bounds of "acceptable" behavior, or even outside the bounds of reality. You can break taboos and enjoy forbidden feelings like lust, aggression, or power. You can even change your gender or sexual orientation in a fantasy. Even while you're having sex with your partner, you can enjoy the thrills of "bad" or "impossible" thoughts while soaking in the physical closeness of lovemaking. Best of all, you don't have to worry about whether she is judging you for these thoughts, because she doesn't have to know about them. All she will know is that you are physically in her arms, getting very sexually excited.

The excitement most of us feel in a new relationship has a lot to do with the unknown: *What's she thinking? What does she like? How does she act in bed? How will I feel when she touches me?* As we learn the answers to these questions, we feel more connected, more comfortable, and less sexual. After some time in a stable relationship, many women say, "I feel like I've lost myself." It's hard to feel excited, to want *more* contact, when you already have too much. We seem to need some distance in order to feel turned on. One way to do that is to bring your most private, erotic thoughts into your physical relationship.

If it feels right, you can decide to tell your partner what's going on in your erotic imagination. But there are some dangers in sharing fantasies. On the one hand, talking about each other's fantasies can deepen trust. On the other hand, it can be a set-up for feeling ashamed or hurt. Most women feel vulnerable sharing information like this, and there's too much potential for a hurtful, judgmental reaction that could make you want to shut down and close up. It's important to have a good sense of how your partner is likely to react before going out on that limb.

It's also important to check your own motivation for talking to your partner about your sexual fantasies. Are you hoping that telling her will relieve some of your guilt for fantasizing or for keeping a secret from her? Or because you assume she'll get turned on by the same fantasy? Neither is a good reason. For one thing, you may feel even more guilty if she acts shocked and disgusted by something that you find stimulating. If guilt is the motivation, try exploring it on your own first. For instance, writing about it in a very private journal or talking with a trusted therapist may help clarify your feelings. It's just not a good idea to expect your partner to help relieve your guilt. She can't be objective, and she has her own feelings to deal with.

There's also the danger that talking about a fantasy will decrease its potency. In that vein, some sex therapists suggest that you share some fantasies but keep some to yourself. Perhaps sharing one fantasy, and seeing how that affects you and your partner, is the best way to decide whether to continue sharing. There's no need for us to know everything about each other, and in fact, it's probably best that we don't. Having thoughts and ideas that are completely private is just another way of ensuring that you keep enough separateness in your relationship. Both of you are entitled to a secret fantasy life. That's what can give you more excitement to bring to the bedroom, where your partner can enjoy it too.

I think that in our understandable longing for intimacy and connection, we often forget something. A little separateness helps you feel sexual! Successful long-term lovers never forget this. Instead, they find a way to meet opposing needs for connection and separateness. In that sense, erotic imagination is an excellent bridge.

Your Turn

Following are some questions about your own erotic imagination. Your answers should be private. If you really do want to share your responses with your partner, make sure you've thought about it carefully, and first read this chapter thoroughly.

① Do you remember one of your first sexual fantasies? What was it? Do you remember how you felt about using fantasy and how you explained it to yourself?

② If you wanted to get really turned on but were afraid you couldn't, what fantasy would be most likely to help you get there?

③ What do you think makes this fantasy so exciting for you? Something random or something that makes sense for you personally?

④ How do you feel about using this fantasy? Any conflicts? If so, describe them.

⑤ What do you imagine would happen if you shared these responses with a partner? Would that be an outcome you would like?

12

Orgasm: Taking Your Time

IT'S HARD TO know these days how much importance to place on orgasm. On the one hand, we hear that we should simply focus on the pleasurable feelings occurring during sex and stop being so goal-oriented about orgasms. We hear that we can miss out on a lot of pleasurable possibilities by the rush to reach the finish line. We hear that relaxing about the outcome could help us enjoy the process of sexual intimacy more. We hear that lovemaking should be like music or dance—that it's about the process, not the grand finale.

However, as a client of mine once said, "Lovemaking without climax is like going to a great theater performance and missing the last act." Anyone can handle an orgasmless experience occasionally, but not all the time. It's just too disappointing, on several levels. Physically, there's all that built-up tension, and no release. Men call it "blue balls." Women may be less crass about it, but many talk about an uncomfortable aching genital sensation. Emotionally, there's often a feeling of personal inadequacy or even failure, bringing up thoughts like, *What's wrong with me?* Often, there's disappointment, because an orgasm can be such an ultimate bonding experience with a partner, and it's sad to miss out on that. Sometimes the disappointment is channeled into irritation with a partner for not giving adequate stimulation. These negative reactions are not fun and don't contribute to more positive feelings about oneself or one's partner. That's the problem about sex without orgasm, and it might supersede the problem of too much focus on orgasm.

Both ways of looking at it do have their strongpoints. And I know that worrying about having an orgasm can really interfere with enjoying sexual intimacy. At the same time, some women are too easily discouraged by difficulties and give up too quickly. It does, after all, feel really good, and there's no reason to deprive oneself of this unique pleasure. To many women, orgasm is an over-rated muscle spasm that gets far too much emphasis, and they don't like the pressure they sometimes feel to produce an orgasm with every sexual encounter. That's true, but let's face it: Given a choice, most women would rather have orgasms than not.

Sandy volunteered to participate in my 2007 survey and follow-up interviews because she had a lot of feelings about her sexual relationships. As she talked, what emerged was that orgasm had been a very negative issue in her previous relationship. She had been with Leslie for seven years . . . and faked orgasm all seven of those years. I asked her how she wound up in this pattern. She said she felt embarrassed because Leslie had orgasms so fast. When Leslie made love to her, Sandy would quickly begin to worry that she was taking too long. She would fake orgasm "to get it over with." After doing this a few times, Sandy was afraid to tell Leslie the truth. Then she felt stuck with faking. This continued for the seven years they were

>

together. They broke up, allegedly, because Sandy wanted to take a job in a new city, but in hindsight, she thought that her sexual frustration was a big cause of her dissatisfaction with the relationship.

I asked Sandy how long she would let Leslie stimulate her before she faked an orgasm. She said "two or three minutes." When I asked her where she got the idea that she should be able to climax that quickly, she said, "I don't know; it seemed so easy for Leslie. I thought it was normal." I explained to her that Leslie was definitely an outlier on the orgasmic speed scale, since most women need about fifteen minutes. Sandy looked shocked and relieved, and talked more about how the push for speed had affected her.

Clearly, Sandy hadn't been taking the time she—and most other women—needed to enjoy the full cycle of arousal and orgasm. Some accurate information about "normal time" for women would have really helped her. But something in their environment added to Sandy's worries about taking too much time. Leslie's parents lived nearby and often dropped in without notice. Both Leslie and Sandy felt like they couldn't count on having privacy for more than a few minutes. When they started making love, there was the unspoken but looming possibility that the doorbell would ring at any minute, and Leslie would feel obliged to answer. This just added to Sandy's feeling that she needed to hurry up.

Listening to Sandy, I felt sad about her seven years of isolation. A little accurate information could have sent her down a different road, where she could have asked Leslie for what she needed, learned how to receive sexual attention and time, and felt more of the wonderful, shared pleasure of orgasm. Instead, she embarked on a pretense that created a chasm between her and her partner. She didn't do this on purpose—she literally didn't know any better.

The interview didn't end on a sad note, however. It turned out that Sandy was just starting to date someone and was on the brink of going to

>

bed with her. She loved knowing that she could expect more time during sex, and that her new partner might need more time also. She also felt relieved to know that it was a good idea to talk about sex and orgasms up front. With more information and less anxiety, Sandy thanked me for the interview and left smiling.

Some women have had orgasms easily all their lives. Others have never experienced one. Most studies have found that at least 20 percent of all women, straight and queer, never have orgasms during sex with a partner.[1] Many women have them occasionally but don't have a sense of what gets them there; it's not really under their control. Some women experience multiple orgasms. Others experience just one orgasm and need a period of relaxation before getting sexually aroused again.

Many women wonder, *How long should it take?* That depends; women are really different in this regard. First, you have to get aroused enough to lubricate, and that can take either no time or forever, depending on the situation. But once that happens, after lubrication starts, some women climax in about three minutes, others in thirty minutes, and most are somewhere in between, with the average being fifteen minutes.[2] The amount of time it takes to orgasm has a great deal to do with anatomy and physiology. We're built differently and have different needs in terms of duration and intensity of stimulation. And because our bodies, minds, and sensitivities are in a state of flux, some women who used to easily reach orgasm find themselves having a harder time of it. When it comes to ease of orgasm for women, nothing is set in stone.

So should you care about whether or not you have orgasms? Yes . . . and no. You should care enough to be informed about them—what they are and how they happen, you should care enough to do your best to find out what brings you to orgasm, and you should care enough to find a way to comfortably communicate with your partner about them. Once armed with those tools, have at it. And if you start to feel anxiety or pressure about it, that's a warning sign that you need to back off. In other words: Familiarize yourself, educate yourself, be able to talk about it . . . and then sit back, relax, and enjoy the show.

So let's start with some demystifying facts about orgasm. Two nerve pathways govern orgasm. The pudendal nerve supplies the clitoris and vulva, while the pelvic nerve goes straight to the vagina and uterus. While some women experience the most sexual pleasure vaginally, many more respond mostly to clitoral stimulation. That's because the pudendal nerve has more sensory fibers than the pelvic nerve. Stimulation of one or both of these nerves leads to a buildup of pleasurable sensations, as well as increasing muscle tension in the pelvic area. As pleasure continues to build, it will reach a peak, and then, if nothing interferes to block the process, it will naturally reverse itself. This reversal is the orgasm: a sudden release of blood that has been accumulating in the pelvic area, as well as a sudden release of muscular tension. In other words, it's a reflex. In fact, physiologically speaking, it's much like a sneeze. How's that for demystification?

When we talk about orgasm in the intimacy workshops, there's usually some laughter about watching the clock during sex. This, of course, can be detrimental to the intimacy. After all, if you're not present, how can you be connected to your partner? I remember, however, one woman who sheepishly admitted she actually had checked the clock once—but it was very helpful for her. For years, she used to worry about taking too long in bed, but then one time she noticed that it was 9:00 P.M. when her partner started touching her, and that it was 9:13 P.M. right after she had an orgasm. She thought, *Oh, thirteen minutes? That's not bad!* Once she had a concrete number in her head, she felt more relaxed and able to focus on enjoying the pleasure her partner was giving her, without the "hurry up" messages in her head.

As I'm sure you've noticed, some people sneeze more readily than others, and most of us sneeze for different reasons. Which makes sense: Everyone has different anatomies and so of course, everyone has a different threshold and different triggers when it comes to sneezing. Same goes for orgasm. We have different thresholds for orgasm, which, for the most part, are determined by our individual anatomies and biologies. This is important to keep in mind, because we tend to compare ourselves to others and judge ourselves for our differences in bed. In particular, women who happen to have a higher threshold than their partners often judge themselves and assume they have psychological "issues" about orgasm. Yes, psychological issues can and sometimes do get in the way of orgasm. But I've seen too many women jump to that type of conclusion without ever really exploring other possibilities, without

getting accurate information, and without ever really trying to practice steps to help themselves reach orgasm.

If we can understand that orgasm is not just a psychological
phenomenon, but also—and mostly—a physiological one, we can
more easily accept ourselves and our differences. After all, you're
not responsible for the size, shape, or precise location of your pudendal and pelvic nerves. You're just born that way. So first make sure
you've done your best to figure out what does carry you across the
threshold. You can resort to psychoanalysis later.

Even if you're not worried about having "issues" related to
arousal and orgasm, many woman are simply worried about duration. Over 50 percent of the women who took my online survey said
they worried about "taking too long."[3] During sex with a partner,
they found themselves wondering, *Will I be able to have an orgasm
this time? How long will it take? Is she getting tired? Bored?* If
my survey's results can be generalized, the majority of women go
through this on a frequent basis. So in a same-sex female couple,
chances are one or both of them are experiencing Orgasm Anxiety.
And of course, anxiety usually makes it more difficult to have an
orgasm, and so it can easily turn into a vicious cycle.

Unfortunately, these feelings lead some women to faking
orgasms. Contrary to popular opinion, women don't just fake with
men—they do it with other women too. A survey of female college
students found that 80 percent had faked orgasms.[4] This was true
for heterosexual and lesbian sexual encounters. One of these students explained, "I'd worry that I was taking too long, and that my
partner would think I had some kind of problem. So I'd just fake it,
and then my partner would feel good about both of us."

FEMALE EJACULATION

A small percentage of women ejaculate one or two tablespoons of clear fluid during orgasm. There's some disagreement about what that percentage is, with some sources saying 20 percent, others 50 percent, and some claiming that 100 percent could, if we all learned how.[A] Regardless of the percentage, we do know that this fluid comes from glands behind the urethra and is pushed out suddenly by the muscle contractions of orgasm.

Most women who experience it say they feel an extra surge of pleasure when they ejaculate during orgasm. In fact, they encourage other women to learn how to ejaculate, by drinking a lot of liquid before sex and by making an effort to urinate at the moment of orgasm. This can produce the ejaculatory response and intensify the pleasure of orgasm.

The phenomenon of female ejaculation draws some mixed reviews. For some women, this is a pleasure worth pursuing. Others are embarrassed, and their partners taken aback, by the orgasmic flood. The embarrassment has to do with a common misconception that the ejaculate is urine. In fact, it is a type of prostrate fluid, with no taste or smell, which is released by some women but not others. The reasons are unknown, but the fact is that for most women this is involuntary.

One client of mine said that she would ejaculate during orgasm with a partner about 20 percent of the time. When she did, she said it was intensely pleasurable, but also embarrassing, because she was afraid of being "too messy." She had been with partners who thought that the fluid was urine, and they seemed shocked and turned off. Regardless, she said, she could neither predict nor control this response, and she did enjoy how good it felt. She was very pleased when she met a woman who was rather intrigued by the process. This woman suggested they keep a towel nearby and showed delight when it happened because she knew it meant extra pleasure.

>

236

Sensitivity and appreciation are important if you or your partner ejaculate during orgasm—sensitivity because so many women are self-conscious about this, and appreciation because it can be an extra source of pleasure. Factual information can also help, as there is widespread misunderstanding of this very natural phenomenon. If either of you are uncomfortable about "being messy," talk with each other about what to anticipate and plan accordingly.

Remember, most women say ejaculation is extremely pleasurable. You may not want to deprive either of you of that extra pleasure. You might also enjoy going online and looking for information on this phenomenon, keeping in mind that there's a great deal of conflicting ideas and very little scientific research about how often this happens.

Unfortunately, a secret like that just widens the gulf between you and your partner and makes you feel more alone and less sexual. It also becomes a habit, one that feeds on itself. Once you start faking, it's hard to stop, so you may feel more upset, enjoy sex even less, and have even more difficulty reaching orgasm. At this point, besides not enjoying sex as much, you can begin to feel a little guilty about deceiving your partner, or even resentful that she's having such a good time and you're not. An overall feelings of helplessness about orgasm can settle in and take over. Fortunately, it doesn't have to be that way.

The best written guide for learning to have orgasms is sex therapist Lonnie Barbach's *For Yourself*. She outlines a step-by-step approach to help you get to know your body better. To give a very abbreviated version: You start with looking at your nude body in a mirror, then you begin touching your own body, gradually moving to touching your own genitals and then specifically stroking your clitoris until you are aroused and eventually, reach orgasm. This is a gradual process, taking several hours a week for several weeks. At each step of the process, the emphasis is on learning to relax and enjoy the sensations, to give yourself positive messages about sexuality, and to figure out which specific kinds of touch are most stimulating for you. Barbach also encourages use of sexual fantasy to increase stimulation and distract you from nonsexual thoughts—for example, more thoughts about a hot sexual scene, fewer thoughts about the grocery list.

This approach to orgasm is the standard recommendation made by sex therapists and is usually called "Directed Masturbation" (DM). Research definitely supports the efficacy of this method. It's been found that over 85 percent of women can learn to have orgasms by practicing masturbation.[5]

Through masturbation, you gradually train your body to respond to sexual stimulation, you learn what you like, and you get more used to feeling sexual pleasure. In a way, learning to have orgasms feels like shooting hoops. First you get the ball in your hands and get oriented toward the basket. Then you dribble toward it, with your own personal rhythm and speed. Then you bring the ball up and release it at a certain point, so it will sail above you and drop into the basket. Obviously, this is a skill that requires development. Without it, you won't get there consistently, if at all. You need practice to figure out which rhythms and speeds work for your body, when to shoot, and when to release the ball. Regular masturbation is regular practice. It gives you a chance to strengthen your sexual response muscles, and to develop a rhythm and flow that carries you over the orgasm threshold. It helps you learn what kinds of stimulation are most exciting, at what point, and how to get that in various forms. Some women like using hands, vibrators, dildos, or a combination of those. The point is to discover what feels the best to you.

ANTIDEPRESSANTS AND ANORGASMIA: THE DEPRESSING TRUTH

There is an unfortunate irony in our widespread use of antidepressant medicine. Depression usually decreases sexual interest. Many antidepressants make people feel better about themselves, so theoretically, they should feel more able to enjoy being sexual. Alas, this is not the case. The cure for one problem can create another one, and antidepressants are a case in point.

The most commonly prescribed antidepressants are SSRIs (selective serotonin reuptake inhibitors). Prozac, Zoloft, Effexor, Paxil, Celexa, Lexipro, and Cymbalta are among the most common. These wonderful medications have brought tremendous relief from depression—and a striking increase in a sense of well-being—to millions of people. Unfortunately, they have major side effects. SSRIs tend to decrease sexual desire, and they can make it difficult—or impossible—to have an orgasm. Researchers from the Kinsey Sex Research Institute estimate that up to 80 percent of people who take SSRIs experience negative sexual side effects, including loss of sexual interest and increased difficulty having an orgasm.[8]

Many women I've seen in my practice have mentioned that they're having more trouble having orgasms than they used to, and they attribute this to their psychological or relationship problems. After I question them

>

a bit more, it often emerges that they have started taking an SSRI and that their doctors did not warn them that orgasmic difficulty is a very common side effect. When I point out the connection, they're usually both relieved and upset by this—relieved because "It's not because there's something wrong with me," and upset because they like feeling less depressed but don't want to give up sexual feelings. Others say it's okay, because they weren't having much sex anyway when they were depressed, so it doesn't feel like that big a loss right now.

In the past, some doctors recommended the "Saturday sex plan": Skip an SSRI dose on Friday and resume it immediately after having sex on Saturday. The sexual side effect usually goes away within 24 hours. Theoretically, with careful planning, you could enjoy a day of feeling more sexual without causing yourself to dip back into a depressive mood. Most psychiatrists do *not* recommend this plan anymore. There may be some risks associated with skipping regular doses, and many people are correctly cautious about altering any prescribed regimen. On the other hand, many women have enjoyed their Saturday sex this way. This is an individual decision that you might want to consider and discuss with whoever prescribes your SSRI.

What psychiatrists are more likely to recommend is a combination of different types of antidepressants. For example, those that affect dopamine more than serotonin can actually enhance sexual feelings and orgasmic potential. There are also some herbal supplements, like gingko biloba, that seem to help sexual sensations by increasing blood flow to the genital area or by increasing testosterone levels temporarily. Some people report that these combinations can help, although nothing works consistently enough to earn the label of "the female Viagra."

The sexual side effects of SSRIs remain an unresolved and unpleasant dilemma, presenting many women with a difficult decision. As I mentioned, some women say they weren't interested in sex anyway, because

>

they were too depressed, so for them, the decision is more straightforward. But other women really struggle with this, and some stop SSRIs abruptly when they realize their sexual functioning is being affected. Stopping abruptly is never, ever a good idea. Many people get extremely irritable or tearful—or worse—when they quit SSRIs suddenly. It's important to talk with a doctor about how to taper off these medications very gradually so you don't put yourself through more distress.

Unfortunately, there are some very negative messages and beliefs that get in the way of masturbation. Some religions condemn it as a sinful activity. Some believe that it's immature or inadequate or selfish to spend time giving yourself pleasure. Many women felt guilty about masturbation when they first started doing it, thinking it was a secret perversion that no one else indulged in; for some of those women, that initial guilt lingers on.

Many feel guilty about masturbation because they think of it as being disloyal to their partners. But it's much more helpful to think of it as priming yourself for partner sex. Research shows that masturbation *helps* people have more sexual satisfaction with a partner. Women who masturbate more also have partner sex more and report more sexual satisfaction in general.[6] Masturbation helps you develop a consistent orgasmic response. (Remember the basketball layups?) It is a very important stepping stone to a more satisfying relationship with a partner. Masturbation helps you learn how to feel optimal sexual pleasure—and these discoveries are what you need to share with your partner.

My survey of lesbian sexual behavior showed an interesting correlation between orgasm and masturbation.[7] A few women said that they never had orgasms during sex with a partner. Of those few, *all* of them also said they never masturbated. So as it turns out, they didn't have orgasms with themselves, either. These women weren't learning about their own sexual responses, so neither were their partners. And that makes sense. After all, you can't transfer knowledge you haven't acquired.

So if you *have* acquired that knowledge, how do you transfer it to your partner? Many women get stuck here: They can have orgasms easily when masturbating, but not with a partner. The key to being orgasmic with a partner is to show her what you've learned about yourself during masturbation. Don't expect that she'll "just know." She won't. You need to show her what is most pleasing to you and help her learn to touch you the way you touch yourself. You can tell her, show her, guide her, whisper to her, write her a note, text her— but you need to let her know. After all, she is a different person than you are, so how would she know what your magic buttons are?

If you remember not to judge yourself about your sexual responses, it will be easier to communicate with your partner—she's probably not going to judge you either. We don't have exactly the same bodies, and we don't need exactly the same kind of stimulation. Again, it's important to understand the implications of different orgasm thresholds. For women with a higher threshold, oral sex might not provide enough intensity to reach orgasm, or the duration needed is more than a partner can comfortably maintain. But remember, there's a balance between expressing what you want and trying to control every move your partner makes. On the television show *The L Word,* there was a very funny scene where a woman gives explicit, nonstop directions to her lover. "Go round and round, faster, not like that, smaller circles, harder, faster, no, like that—not like that—that's it, more—not so hard—keep going. . . ." Not very subtle, and not everyone is blessed with a partner who wouldn't start to feel exasperated by such an onslaught of directives. This is why it's important to understand that you can always mix in a little self-stimulation if your partner isn't hitting all the right notes. That would probably be more arousing to your partner than directing her every move—and she may be able to watch and learn something that will help her next time.

Working together with your partner to deal with challenges related to orgasm can be a wonderful, vulnerable bonding experience. One woman, Victoria, explained it this way. "When we were first lovers, I felt so frustrated because I couldn't have an orgasm with her. Sometimes I'd masturbate alone, after we made love, just so I could get some release. I was crazy about her and felt all this passion, but I just couldn't go over the edge. Finally I told her how much that bothered me, and that I was afraid she would think I had too many sexual problems. But she went and got this book about orgasms. We read some of it together and practiced some of the techniques. I started having orgasms with her, and it was wonderful. I appreciate her so much. Now I'm glad I had that problem, because it made me take risks with her, and she really came through for me. I trust her more than ever."

Victoria's experience was the perfect illustration of the gift of orgasmic difficulties. She was motivated enough to risk telling her partner, and

>

she was wonderfully surprised by her partner's very positive response. This experience set the tone for their relationship. Victoria knew she could trust her partner to hear her, to not judge her, and to take positive action. The fact that she learned this through their sexual relationship added a special dimension that she experienced each time they made love.

Many women help themselves reach orgasm by self-stimulation or using a vibrator during partner sex. This can be a great thing: You can share the intimacy and pleasure with her, enjoy what she does for you, and enjoy what you can do for yourself. Teamwork!

An example of how this can work would be to create an understanding with your partner: She will stimulate you for ten or fifteen minutes, while you simply relax and enjoy it. After that, you'll take over doing whatever helps you reach orgasm. You can masturbate, use a vibrator, whatever you like best. This way your partner can enjoy making love to you without having to worry, *Can I do this long enough? Can I do it well enough?* Likewise, you don't have to worry, *How long am I going to take?* It's a way to incorporate the best both of you have to offer in a good sexual encounter. You're going to have the satisfaction of an orgasm in her arms, without the prior angst.

There can be a hangup here. Some women are hesitant to do something like this because they're fixed on the idea that it's important to be able to "give" your partner an orgasm. Before getting too hung up on that, consider this: Orgasms reached through masturbation are usually more intense than those reached in partner sex. That's because no one else can stimulate you quite as well as you can yourself. Would you want to deprive yourself, and your partner, of more intense pleasure just to prove a point about who's giving what to whom? It's very vulnerable and intimate to let your partner see you bringing yourself to orgasm. There's also a great deal of gratitude to partners who encourage you to have the most satisfying orgasms you can have, however you like to have them. You'll know she's more invested in your pleasure than in her own lovemaking skills, and that's a great foundation for other aspects of your relationship.

Believe it or not, there can be a gift in sexual difficulties, if you choose to accept it. Sometimes our bodies motivate us to take some risks, which can have great payoffs. It takes courage to tell a partner you want to have orgasms with her, to talk about what would help you, and to ask her to experiment with you. That's a pretty vulnerable position to be in, and most of us wouldn't take the risk if there weren't a major incentive—an orgasm! Communicating with each other about orgasmic difficulties leads to a much deeper level of trust and relaxation with each other.

So instead of being mad at your body for not producing an orgasm easily, try to appreciate the opportunity you have to really test out your trust for this partner, and for yourself. The gift in this difficulty is that it forces you both to engage in the kind of positive, sensitive, honest communication that will strengthen every aspect of your relationship. You will appreciate each other in a whole new way, and you'll be reminded of this every time you make love.

Your Turn

These questions invite you first to think about your own experiences, then talk with your partner about yours and hers. When she talks to you, accept what she says graciously. She may like something you hate—you're two different people! And that's a good thing, when it comes to sex.

① Think about your own experiences with orgasm. Do you remember your first orgasm or (if you don't have them) your first efforts to have one? What do you think you learned from those? Were these positive or negative experiences? Do you see some ways those experiences still affect you today?

② If you have orgasms today, what helps you have them most easily? And how open are you with partners about this? What kinds of reactions have you had from partners if/when you talked about orgasm?

③ Can you talk with your partner about these questions and find out about her experiences?

④ Write down what you'd like your partner to know about what helps you have orgasms most easily. Ask her to do the same. Then read your lists to each other—don't talk about it, just read. Tell each other you can talk about it in 24 hours; for now, just read and listen.

⑤ If it's too hard to write a list, think about what would make this easier for you. Is there something your partner could do that would make you feel more comfortable than sharing a list like this? Also ask her what you can do that would help her feel most comfortable. Then set up a time, and do it.

Epilogue

When I first fell in love with a woman, I was head over heels . . . and wracked with fear. I felt thrilled to know the truth about myself, but I was afraid of the consequences. How would I tell my family and friends? Would they think I was perverted? Mentally ill?

It was a piece of wisdom from the Bible, of all places, that came to my rescue: "Perfect love casts out fear." That short, sweet verse gave me the courage I needed to let my newfound joy flourish, despite my many worries about this major life change.

If you are seeking to change your sexual relationship with your partner, both of you will need some courage. Luckily, you have each other. And though it will surely be a challenging, bumpy road from time to time, the journey can be a bonding adventure, and the destination—a satisfying sex life with your lover—makes the trip entirely worthwhile.

Any significant change, whether it is intentionally invited into our lives or not, always comes with a good deal of anxiety. After all, change means entering into an unknown territory, and that, of course, has an unnerving affect on us. But it's during such experiences that we are also blessed with a heightened awareness. We are more alert, alive, and aware than ever, and this is when we have the most opportunity for personal growth and wisdom.

If you're reading this book, you've already shown some courage: You've been curious about some "forbidden" topics, and you've been willing to consider different ways to deepen sexual intimacy in your own relationship. In many ways, that first leg of this journey is the scariest. Not everyone makes it this far. Many partnered women, instead of rocking the love boat, just coast along, living very contented albeit virtually celibate lives.

Sometimes, that's fine. As I've been writing this book I've been asked—frequently—if I'm passing judgment on women who love their partners but don't care to have sex with them. Absolutely not. If both partners are on the same page about sex, there's no problem. My point, however, is that some women have not given this important facet of life the thought it deserves. Or perhaps they have but eventually gave in to inertia, complacency, or the desire to avoid conflict.

The fact that this book is in your hands shows that you do not fall into this category. You have chosen to lean into the discomfort, to take a risk, to improve your life in a very personal and very important way.

Your courage is the catalyst, and when coupled with patience, openness, and knowledge, I believe you will be successful in your endeavors to deepen your communication and your sexual intimacy with your partner.

But I hope it doesn't stop there. Once you've joined the ranks of the sexually active, I invite you to invite others to do the same. As I've said before, too many women *don't* lean into the discomfort . . . or never even think to try. You have to power to change that, to inspire others to follow your suit, and you can wield that power simply by talking more about sex and desire within your circles.

Epilogue

Yes, we've told the world that we're here and we're queer, but now it's time to talk to each other.

I realize that this is going to take some getting used to. Though it's slowly getting easier for us to celebrate our sexual *orientation*, it's still not easy for us to celebrate our sexuality. Often, we're encouraged not to discuss sex at all. Years ago, soon after I came out, I talked with a professor who had joined Parents, Families, and Friends of Lesbians and Gays (PFLAG) as a way to support her lesbian daughter. During our brief conversation, she asked me a question that stuck with me for a long time. She said, "Why do lesbians have to talk about sex so much? Every time you do, I have to explain to my friends that it's not really about the sex, it's about the emotional intimacy." She described different times when she had attempted to defuse negative judgments about same-sex relationships by minimizing sex and maximizing companionship. This professor was obviously sincere and caring, and I knew she was trying to protect her daughter from antigay hostility. Her words stayed with me, but not for the reasons she intended.

What she was essentially saying was, "Don't talk about sex." But if it's not about sex, then what is it about?

I have friends I feel really close to, but I don't have sex with them. And I don't really think society, or my extended family, would care if I just had same-sex "companions." The negative judgment isn't about emotional intimacy. It's about the sex. The sex is what makes us different, and we ourselves need to recognize that.

In these modern times, making sexual satisfaction an acceptable goal in our community may seem completely obvious, a no-brainer.

But that doesn't mean it's going to be a piece of cake. In many ways, we need to go against the very grain of our basic cultural training.

Put simply, pleasure is a worthy goal that all people are entitled to enjoy. But this country was founded on the Puritan work ethic, and deep down, I think Americans still have ingrained in them the notion that the pursuit of pleasure for its own sake is wrong, shallow, selfish, or a distraction from what should be important in life. If you've ever felt guilty for reading a magazine when there were dishes to be washed, you may have an inkling of what I mean. If you decide you're not going to enjoy yourself until everything else is taken care of, you never will. There will *always* be more dirty dishes, more floors to sweep, more laundry to do. As long as you're alive, there will always be an unfinished to-do list.

But depriving yourself of pleasure doesn't help anyone else, or improve conditions in the world, or produce more needed goods and services. Self-deprivation just mean you go through life with less joy. And people with less joy have less to give to others. The most generous thing you can do—not only for yourself, but also for the world around you—is to put your best foot forward toward your own personal happiness.

The trick, though, is negotiating your own personal happiness with that of your partner. That's where communication and respect for individual differences come in. You and your lover are, after all, two different people. You have different bodies and minds, and you respond to sexual stimuli in different ways. She may take more or less time to get aroused, or to orgasm. Maybe you like erotica but she doesn't. She may like complete nudity but you might like to keep a shirt on. You may be quiet; she may be loud. There are many, many ways to be different from each other, and all these ways are equally valid and valuable.

But sexual differences can be particularly challenging to accept without judgments or comparisons. It's hard to undo years of negative training from our families, religion, cultural traditions, and maybe even our sexual partners. Even the field of psychology has done some damage, in my opinion. There is a wealth of negative labels—such as "inhibited," "repressed," "compulsive," or "addictive"—but very few words to describe "healthy" variations in sexual functioning. In a way, Puritanism has joined hands with modern psychology, only the idea of "sex as sin" has been replaced with "sex as pathology" . . . with the same destructive result.

We have the power to change that. By talking more freely about our sexual intimacy and desire, we not only spread the truth, but we also "normalize" the healthy range of differences we all have, as well as the topic itself. Here's an analogy. For most intents and purposes, we don't consider a word "real" unless it is in the dictionary. But every edition of a dictionary is different from the last, with newly added and newly deleted words. And why? Because lexicographers careful study the language as it is used. In other words, *we* are the ones who decide what's in the dictionary. In the same way, we too are the ones who decide what is normal, acceptable, encouraged, and discouraged in our society.

It's time to dispel the myths; to talk about desire, orgasms, hormones, frequency of sexual relations. It's time to stop whispering about lesbian bed death and start talking about our sex lives. Doing so will encourage other women to open up and do the same—and perhaps, if we start talking about it enough, we will spark more interest in the research communities to do the much needed studies about sex between women.

If you ever start to doubt whether you can continue on this path toward more passion with your partner, look back at where you've already been. Your journey started when you expressed sexual love for a woman. Your passion and courage were strong enough to override a lifetime of programming, and those same wonderful feelings can help you get back on track today. Because today, you're more powerful than you were when you started. You know about avoidance and sexual silence—but you also have the experience and knowledge to help you meet the challenge of changing those old patterns, and you know what sexual intimacy brings into your life. So congratulate yourself on how far you've already traveled, keep talking, and keep walking toward that passionate light.

Endnotes

Introduction

1 Glenda Corwin and Maggie Fotiadis, "Sexual Behavior Patterns among Lesbian Couples" (poster presented at Southeastern Psychology Conference, Charlotte, NC, 2008).

/

1 Philip Blumstein and Pepper Schwartz, *American Couples* (New York: William Morrow, 1983), 316–317.

2 Marny Hall, "Lesbians, Limerence, and Long-Term Relationships," in *Lesbian Sex,* by J. Loulan (San Francisco: Spinsters Ink, 1984), 141–150.

3 Suzanne Iasenza, "Lesbian Sexuality Post-Stonewall to Postmodernism: Putting the 'Lesbian Bed Death' Concept to Bed," *Journal of Sex Education and Therapy* 24, no. 1 (2000): 61.

4 Barry McCarthy and Emily McCarthy, *Rekindling Desire* (New York: Brunner-Routledge, 2003), 5–6.

5 Glenda Corwin and Maggie Fotiadis, "Sexual Behavior Patterns among Lesbian Couples" (poster presented at Southeastern Psychology Conference, Charlotte, NC, 2008).

6 Edward Laumann, Anthony Paik, and Raymond Rosen, "Sexual Dysfunction in the United States: Prevalence and

Predictors," *Journal of the American Medical Association* 281, no. 6 (1999): 537–544.

7   Laumann, et al., "Sexual Problems among Women and Men Aged 40–80 Years: Prevalence and Correlates Identified in the Global Study of Sexual Attitudes and Behaviors," *International Journal of Impotence Research* 17 (2005): 39–57.

8   Cindy M. Meston and Julia R. Heiman, "Sexual Abuse and Sexual Function: An Examination of Sexually Relevant Cognitive Processes," *Journal of Counseling and Clinical Psychology* 68, no. 3 (2000): 399–406.

9   Glenda Corwin and Maggie Fotiadis, "Sexual Behavior Patterns among Lesbian Couples" (poster presented at Southeastern Psychology Conference, Charlotte, NC, 2008).

10 Barry McCarthy and Emily McCarthy, *Rekindling Desire* (New York: Brunner-Routledge, 2003).

2

1   Marny Hall, "Lesbians, Limerence, and Long-Term Relationships," in *Lesbian Sex,* by J. Loulan (San Francisco: Spinsters Ink, 1984).

2   Helen Fisher, *Why We Love: The Nature and Chemistry of Romantic Love* (New York: Henry Holt, 2004).

3   Pat Love and Jo Robinson, *Hot Monogamy: Essential Steps to More Passionate, Intimate Lovemaking* (New York: Plume, 1994).

4 Helen Fisher, *Why We Love: The Nature and Chemistry of Romantic Love* (New York: Henry Holt, 2004).

5 Martin Seligman, *Learned Optimism* (New York: Random House, 1998).

6 Pat Love and Jo Robinson, *Hot Monogamy: Essential Steps to More Passionate, Intimate Lovemaking* (New York: Plume, 1994).

7 Donald Dutton and Arthur Aron, "Some Evidence of Heightened Sexual Attraction under Conditions of High Anxiety," *Journal of Personality and Social Psychology* 30, no. 4 (1974): 510–517.

8 Jack Morin, *The Erotic Mind: Unlocking the Inner Sources of Sexual Passion and Fulfillment* (New York: HarperCollins, 1995).

9 K. L. Falco, in Kathleen Ritter and Anthony Terndrup, *Handbook of Affirmative Psychotherapy with Lesbians and Gay Men* (New York: Guilford Press, 2002), 5.

10 Barry McCarthy, "Protecting Marriage" (workshop presented in Atlanta, 2007).

11 Rosemary Basson, "Using a Different Model for Female Sexual Response to Address Women's Problematic Low Sexual Desire," *Journal of Sex and Marital Therapy* 27 (2001): 395–403.

12 David Goldmeir, "Responsive Sexual Desire in Women—Managing the Normal?" *Sexual and Relationship Therapy* 16, no. 4 (2001): 381–387.

3

1 Laumann, et al., "Sexual Problems among Women and Men Aged 40–80 Years: Prevalence and Correlates Identified in the Global Study of Sexual Attitudes and Behaviors," *International Journal of Impotence Research* 17 (2005): 39–57.

4

1 Antronette K. Yancey and others, "Correlates of Overweight and Obesity among Lesbian and Bisexual Women," *Preventive Medicine* 36 (2003): 676–683.

2 Pipher, Mary, *Reviving Ophelia: Saving the Selves of Adolescent Girls* (New York: Ballantine Books, 1994).

3 Ulrike Boehmer, Debora Bowen, and Greta Bauer, "Overweight and Obesity in Sexual Minority Women: Evidence from Population-Based Data," *American Journal of Public Health* 97, no. 6 (2007): 1134–1140.

5

1 Judith Herman, *Trauma and Recovery* (New York: Basic Books, 1992).

2 John Briere, "Treatment of Post-Traumatic Stress Disorder" (workshop presented for Division E, Georgia Psychological Association, Ashville, NC, January 2005).

3 Cindy Meston, Julia Heiman, and Paul Trapnell, "The Relation between Early Abuse and Adult Sexuality," *Journal of Sex Research* 36, no. 4 (1999): 385.

4 Jeanne Shaw, personal communication, 2008.

6

1 Christiane Northrup, *The Wisdom of Menopause: Creating Physical and Emotional Health During the Change* (New York: Bantam Books, 2006), 276–303.

2 Ernest Becker, *The Denial of Death* (New York: Free Press, 1973).

3 David Schnarch, *Passionate Marriage* (New York: Henry Holt, 1997).

4 Edward Laumann, Anthony Paik, and Raymond Rosen, "Sexual Dysfunction in the United States: Prevalence and Predictors," *Journal of the American Medical Association* 281, no. 6 (1999): 537–544; and Laumann, et al., "Sexual Problems among Women and Men Aged 40–80 Years: Prevalence and Correlates Identified in the Global Study of Sexual Attitudes and Behaviors," *International Journal of Impotence Research* 17 (2005): 39–57.

5 Beverley Johnson, "Older Women Talking about Sex," *Selfhelp Magazine.* www.selfhelpmagazine.com/article /elder-sex. Originally published May 13, 1998, revised September 3, 2008 by Marlene M. Maheu.

6 Ibid.

7 Glenda Corwin and Maggie Fotiadis, "Sexual Behavior Patterns among Lesbian Couples" (poster presented at Southeastern Psychology Conference, Charlotte, NC, 2008).

8 Christiane Northrup, *The Wisdom of Menopause: Creating Physical and Emotional Health During the Change* (New York: Bantam Books, 2006).

9 Ibid.

10 Jen Johnsen, MD, personal communication, 2009.

7

1 Don-David Lusterman, *Infidelity: A Survival Guide* (Oakland, CA: New Harbinger, 1998), 21.

2 Dana Truman-Schram and others, "Leaving an Abusive Relationship: An Investment Model of Women Who Stay versus Women Who Leave," *Journal of Social and Clinical Psychology* 19, no. 2 (2000): 163.

A "Compersion," http://en.wikipedia.org/wiki/Compersion.

B Hara Estroff Marano, "Jealousy: Love's Destroyer," *Psychology Today* 42, no. 4 (2009): 62–68.

C William Rock, "Jealousy and the Abyss," *Journal of Humanistic Psychology* 23, no. 2 (1983): 70–84.

8

1 Lynda Dykes Talmadge and William Talmadge, *Love Making: The Intimate Journey in Marriage* (St. Paul: Syren Book Company, 2004).

2 Glenda Corwin and Maggie Fotiadis, "Sexual Behavior Patterns among Lesbian Couples" (poster presented at Southeastern Psychology Conference, Charlotte, NC, 2008).

3 Minuchin, Salvador, *Families and Family Therapy* (New York: Basic Books, 1977).

9

A   Kathleen Morrow and J. Allsworth, "Sexual Risk in Lesbian and Bisexual Women," *Journal of the Gay and Lesbian Medical Association,* no. 4 (2000): 159–165.

B   Ibid.

C   Ibid.

10

1   Philip Blumstein and Pepper Schwartz, *American Couples* (New York: William Morrow, 1983), 316–317.

11

1   Barry McCarthy and Emily McCarthy, *Rekindling Desire* (New York: Brunner-Routledge, 2003), 149.

2   Pat Love and Jo Robinson, *Hot Monogamy: Essential Steps to More Passionate, Intimate Lovemaking* (New York: Plume, 1994), 247.

3   Bergner, Daniel. "What Do Women Want?" *New York Times Magazine,* January 25, 2009, 30.

4   Meredith Chivers and others, "A Sex Difference in the Specificity of Sexual Arousal," *Psychological Sciences* 15, no. 11 (2004): 736–744.

McCarthy, Barry, and Emily McCarthy. *Rekindling Desire: A Step-by-Step Program to Help Low-Sex and No-Sex Marriages.* New York: Brunner-Routledge, 2003.

Meana, Marta, Remie Spicer Rakipi, Gerald Weeks, and Amy Lykins. "Sexual Functioning in a Non-Clinical Sample of Partnered Lesbians." *Journal of Couple & Relationship Therapy* 5, no. 2 (2006): 1–22.

Meston, Cindy M., and Julia R. Heiman. "Sexual Abuse and Sexual Function: An Examination of Sexually Relevant Cognitive Processes." *Journal of Counseling and Clinical Psychology* 68, no. 3 (2000): 399–406.

Meston, Cindy M., Julia R. Heiman, and Paul D. Trapnell. "The Relation between Early Abuse and Adult Sexuality." *The Journal of Sex Research* 36, no. 4 (1999): 385–395.

Miletski, Hami. "Member Spotlight: Interview with Margaret Nichols," *Contemporary Sexuality* 40, no. 9 (2006): 3.

Minuchin, Salvador. *Families and Family Therapy.* New York: Basic Books, 1977.

Morin, Jack. *The Erotic Mind: Unlocking the Inner Sources of Sexual Passion and Fulfillment.* New York: HarperCollins, 1995.

Morrow, Kathleen and J. Allsworth. "Sexual Risk in Lesbian and Bisexual Women." *Journal of the Gay and Lesbian Medical Association* 4 (2000): 159–165.

Newman, Felice. *The Whole Lesbian Sex Book: A Passionate Guide for All of Us.* San Francisco: Cleis Press, 1999.

Northrup, Christiane. *The Wisdom of Menopause: Creating Physical and Emotional Health During the Change.* New York: Bantam Books, 2006.

Perel, Esther. *Mating in Captivity: Reconciling the Erotic and the Domestic.* New York: HarperCollins, 2006.

Pipher, Mary. *Reviving Ophelia: Saving the Selves of Adolescent Girls.* New York: Ballantine Books, 1994.

Post, Laura L., and Judith E. Avery. "Therapeutic Approaches to Inhibited Sexual Desire in Lesbians." *Counseling Psychology Quarterly* 8, no. 3 (1995): 213–220.

Ritter, Kathleen Y., and Anthony I. Terndrup. *Handbook of Affirmative Psychotherapy with Lesbians and Gay Men.* New York: Guilford Press, 2002.

Roach, Mary. *Bonk: The Curious Coupling of Science and Sex.* New York: W.W. Norton, 2008.

Rock, William. "Jealousy and the Abyss," *Journal of Humanistic Psychology* 23, no. 2 (1983): 70–84.

Schloredt, Kelly A., and Julia R. Heiman. "Perceptions of Sexuality as Related to Sexual Functioning and Sexual Risk in Women with Different Types of Childhood Abuse Histories," *Journal of Traumatic Stress* 16, no. 3 (2003): 275–284.

Schnarch, David. *Passionate Marriage: Keeping Love and Intimacy Alive in Committed Relationships.* New York: Henry Holt, 1997.

Seligman, Martin. *Learned Optimism.* New York: Random House, 1998.

Stendhal, Renate. *True Secrets of Lesbian Desire: Keeping Sex Alive in Long-Term Relationships.* Berkeley: North Atlantic Books, 2003.

Truman-Schram, Dana, Arnie Cann, Lawrence Calhoun, and Lori Vanwallendael. "Leaving an Abusive Dating Relationship:

Acknowledgments

I WANT TO thank my mentor and former professor, Dr. Pauline Rose Clance, for her encouragement to write this book, and for many years of wise guidance. Like so many others who have been privileged to work with her, I feel fortunate to have her support.

My deep appreciation also goes to my friend and colleague Dr. Eileen Cooley, who generously shared her clear thinking, research expertise, and enthusiasm for this project. I'm also grateful to my friend Marsha Bond, who patiently read so many chapters and offered her balanced perspective. Marie Josette Murray and Chris Lahowitch also gave me their insightful and much-appreciated feedback.

A heartfelt thanks to my editor, Wendy Taylor (who worked with Krista Lyons at Seal Press) for her clarity, focus, and her kind patience throughout this process. Her assistance has been invaluable.

Of all those who have helped me, I'm most grateful to the many women who shared their personal thoughts and stories with me. Their courage and honesty are what made this book possible. They have my deepest respect.

About the Author

GLENDA CORWIN, PHD, is a clinical psychologist who has been in private practice for more than twenty years. She provides gay-affirmative psychotherapy, and consults with professionals and the general public on sexual issues for women in same-sex relationships. Dr. Corwin leads weekend sexual intimacy workshops for women, and in 2007 conducted a research project investigating lesbian sexual patterns. The very positive responses to her workshops and research were the inspiration for this book.

The daughter of missionaries, Dr. Corwin grew up in Colombia, South America. Her background gives her a deep appreciation for diversity of cultures, languages, and human connections. She also appreciates the lovely woman who shares her life in Atlanta.

For more information about Dr. Corwin and her work, visit her website at www.DrGlendaCorwin.com.

Selected Titles from Seal Press

For more than thirty years, Seal Press has published groundbreaking books.
By women. For women. Visit our website at www.sealpress.com.
Check out the Seal Press blog at www.sealpress.com/blog.

Lesbian Couples: A Guide to Creating Healthy Relationships, by D. Merilee Clunis and G. Dorsey Green. $16.95, 978-1-58005-131-6. Drawing from a decade of research, this helpful and readable resource covers topics from conflict-resolution to commitment ceremonies, using a variety of examples and problem-solving techniques.

Sexier Sex: Lessons from the Brave New Sexual Frontier, by Regina Lynn. $14.95, 978-1-58005-231-3. A fun, provocative guide to discovering your sexuality and getting more pleasure from your sensual life.

The Choice Effect: Love and Commitment in an Age of Too Many Options, by Amalia McGibbon, Lara Vogel, and Claire A. Williams. $16.95, 978-1-58005-293-1. Three young, successful, and ambitious women provide insight into the quarterlife angst that surrounds dating and relationships and examine why more options equals less commitment for today's twentysomethings.

Good Porn: A Woman's Guide, by Erika Lust. $17.95, 978-1-58005-306-8. Fun, fact-filled, and totally racy, *Good Porn* is an unapologetic celebration of porn—and a guide both for women who like it and those who don't know what they're missing.

Valencia, by Michelle Tea. $14.95, 978-1-58005-238-2. A fast-paced account of one girl's search for love and high times in the dyke world of San Francisco. By turns poetic and frantic, Valencia is a visceral ride through the queer girl underground of the Mission.

Girl in Need of a Tourniquet: A Borderline Personality Memoir, by Merri Lisa Johnson. $16.95, 978-1-58005-305-1. This riveting and dramatic personal account gives us a glimpse of what it means to have borderline personality disorder and be in a relationship.